FRED CRAWFORD AND FIFTY GOLDEN YEARS OF PHILANTHROPY

by
James C. Hardie

1663 LIBERTY DRIVE, SUITE 200
BLOOMINGTON, INDIANA 47403
(800) 839-8640
WWW.AUTHORHOUSE.COM

© 2005 James C. Hardie. All Rights Reserved.

No part of this book may be reproduced, stored in a retrieval system, or transmitted by any means without the written permission of the author.

First published by AuthorHouse 05/17/05

ISBN: 1-4208-2716-2 (hc)

Printed in the United States of America
Bloomington, Indiana

This book is printed on acid-free paper.

Cover design by Em (Mrs. J.C.) Hardie

Dedicated to

Mrs. Frederick C. (Kay) Crawford

SOME PEER COMMENTS

Many years have passed since 1968 when Jim Hardie hired me to serve on his development staff at Case Western Reserve University. Over the years he has been a willing counselor and friend, as I passed through various career moves.

In this book, Jim shares his experiences and understanding that philanthropy would not succeed without the dedicated efforts of devoted volunteers. Jim's keen insights and knowledge of the motivation that drove people's generosity to support charitable institutions came from his ability to assimilate information and learn from the volunteers he guided.

His book reminded me of all those great men and women, dedicated in service to others, who exemplified themselves with their gifts of philanthropy and wisdom. And, I am grateful that I was a recipient of that heritage.

James Joseph, executive development specialist; award winning faculty member, Chillicothe Community College; and former Public Relations Director, Mead Paper Co.

~~~~~~~~~~~~~~~~~~~~~~~

Jim illustrates, through numerous humorous and fascinating stories, how dedicated and visionary volunteer leadership helped shape a regional economy. His book is a case study on leveraging resources and is as relevant as ever.

The effective time-honored process begins with the power of one person's philanthropic commitment to an idea. Others are compelled to follow this lead and, in the process, create opportunities for new ideas and community leaders to emerge.

Mick Latkovich, Vice President, Organization and Resource Development, Vocational Guidance Services (VGS)

~~~~~~~~~~~~~~~~~~~~~~~~

Fred Crawford was a visionary leader in business and in philanthropy. Much of what we enjoy today emanating from the Cleveland area's major non-profit institutions is as a result of his business and volunteer leadership over the last half of the twentieth century.

During the time of Crawford's visionary leadership, Jim Hardie transformed the best development practices and taught them to an entire generation of development professionals and volunteers who emulated the qualities of his colleague and friend.

Every development professional who values vision, ethics, leadership and who truly loves this field of study and practice should own a copy of *Fred Crawford and Fifty Golden Years of Philanthropy*.

August A. Napoli, Jr., Vice Chairman, Division of Institutional Relations and Development, The Cleveland Clinic Foundation

Contents

Preface 1

The Fifty Golden Years 3

Summation 149

Individuals Mentioned in the Book 153

PREFACE

This book is the result of my 50 years of work in the philanthropic area, mostly in Northeast Ohio. It is also a tribute to Fred Crawford and the philanthropic leaders with whom I was associated for most of those years.

When Kermit Pike, associate director of the Western Reserve Historical Society, asked me to give my records to the Society so that they could be used as a basis for a new philanthropic archive, which the Society was initiating under the direction of archivest-historian Margaret Bays, I agreed to do so. I also said that I would write a book covering what I called "Fifty Golden Years of Philanthropy in Cleveland and Fred Crawford's Influence."

During those "Fifty Golden Years" I was vice president of Case Institute and Case Western Reserve and a fundraising development consultant to more than 60 northeastern Ohio institutions, some for as long as 20 years and others for as many as five different time periods. In addition, I met with more than 200 non-profit institutions to advise them relative to their philanthropic needs and plans.

It is difficult to separate the fundraising techniques and methods I developed and used from the volunteer leaders, such as Fred Crawford, who were vital to my success and the success of the philanthropic efforts I helped organize.

"People give to people, not to causes" became a truism which I repeated often to underscore the fact that I didn't "ask" for the gifts myself -- the trustees and other interested friends of the institutions were the "askers." I just told them how to do it and gave them the "ammunition" for success.

Through the years I used interesting and humorous stories about Fred Crawford, Charlie White, Jim Lincoln, Kent Smith and other well-known community leaders to illustrate the points I was making to fundraising volunteers, and motivate them to go out and do likewise. Most people don't like to ask others to give, but they do because, as Charlie White said, "If I don't do it, it won't get done."

James C. Hardie

Numerous people over the years encouraged me to write a book including these "stories" so I have included both the "stories" and the history of the development of the Fifty Golden Years of Cleveland Philanthropy in one book. I have melded the "stories" and the philanthropic methodology which I helped develop.

THE FIFTY GOLDEN YEARS

I arrived in Cleveland in January of 1957 to be director of development at Case Institute of Technology where Fred Crawford was chairman of the board.

Over the next four decades of Fred's life I was vice president of Case and Case Western Reserve University and then I served as a fundraising consultant to more than 60 Northeastern Ohio institutions, which raised hundreds of millions of dollars, making the Cleveland area one of the country's premier philanthropic areas. I believe that Fred Crawford influenced Cleveland's remarkable record more than any other person.

He was one of the nation's most exciting speakers; he was ready to back anyone who wanted to do something important for our community; he was fun to be with; he was keenly interested in everyone he came in contact with -- waitresses, caddies, machinists, and so forth, and wanted to find out about them. They were "diamonds" to be explored. They immediately knew that he was sincerely interested in them and they loved him.

Fred Crawford made more people happy than any man I have ever met.

Fred Crawford raised the community's entire philanthropic level, making it fun to attend fundraising kickoffs, fundraising report meetings, and other related fundraising functions where he was involved. This book is a memorial to Fred and to the other leaders who stepped up to the front in this golden era, often because of Fred Crawford's influence.

Many people thought that I wrote Fred Crawford's speeches, but this is not true. He had spent 20 years making speeches in his early career and, because he had a brilliant computer (his brain), he was able to pull out pieces of those speeches and use them. For example, when Case received a $9 million grant from the Ford Foundation, which at that time was one of the largest gifts made in Cleveland and probably one of the largest made in the country, with the help of Clevelander George Humphrey, who was secretary of the treasury under Eisenhower and because of Fred's relationship with Eisenhower, we arranged to have a dinner meeting for a thousand people at Case to announce the gift and asked Eisenhower to make some comments. He agreed. The president of Case, Keith Glennan, said to me, "You run the meeting and we'll have everyone at Case report to you, including me." Fred was the master of ceremonies.

As the people were gathering for the meeting I was standing off to the side with some of Cleveland's most influential people when Fred jauntily came into the area and said, "Jim, what do you want me to say?" I said, "Fred, give them 'the Plymouth Rock' -- Mayflower piece." (His mother's family were Mayflower descendants.) He pulled out an envelope and wrote "Plymouth." Then I said, "Give them the 'importance of education' pitch." And he wrote "education." I said, "How about the greatness of America." He wrote that down. And then I said, "End with alliteration." And he wrote "alliteration." Many of the leaders standing there might have come to the conclusion that I was writing his speech but it was just that I knew him so well and I knew how his mind functioned. Also, I'm certain that he had thought about his remarks on the way to the meeting.

We arranged for the meeting to be on television and the director from the television station said we would be "live" at 7:30 and we should try to finish at 8:00. I mentioned these times to Fred and without much preparation or any great plans about timing, I signaled to him to begin at 7:30. At 8:00 he concluded his remarks and turned to me and winked. It worked out perfectly. (A tape of the meeting, including Ike's important comments, is probably in the Case archives.)

An interesting sideline is that as we waited for the meeting and the thousand people were assembling on the Case campus, Fred Crawford, President Glennan, George Humphrey, "Ike" and I got together at the Wade Park Manor. I had two of my secretaries sitting outside the room we had reserved in the event that Ike needed something. When it came time for us to go to the meeting, Ike grabbed his derby and we started down the hall. We had reached the elevators when Ike stopped abruptly and said, "Oh, I forgot something" and started back down the hall. I followed him. When we got back to the room, the two secretaries were still sitting outside. He stopped in front of them holding his derby in his two hands and bowing slightly said, "Ladies, I don't know what's the matter with me but I was going to leave without thanking you." I can tell you that he had two votes, make that three, including mine. It was a perfect example of the manners of a great gentleman.

Another interesting story about that meeting was that I had set up a sort of central command post where I would be. My excellent staff, with phones, was spread around at various points both in and outside the gym. I had also worked out a liaison arrangement with the catering staff so that there would be no hitches. We started the meeting on time, which was the way all the meetings that I had anything to do with started. In a few minutes there seemed to be some sort of problem. I immediately called the representative from the catering company and asked, "What's happened?" He said, "We can't go on to the next course because Ike hasn't finished his shrimp." I quickly contacted Ike's protocol representative, who was nearby and said that the meeting was being held up because Ike hadn't finished his shrimp. He smiled and said, "Ike doesn't eat shrimp!" So the meeting continued on time.

I did have an opportunity to do a lot of writing for Fred – communications from him to the members of various volunteer committees and other trustees. I never checked thoroughly, but I think he had a master's in engineering from Harvard. While I'm not certain, I think Fred's undergraduate education at that time was the classic Greek-Latin type. He was on the board of one of the two American universities in the Middle East, probably the American University at Athens. I know he treasured a couple of beautiful vases he owned, probably because of that connection. As I did various types of writing for his signature, I noticed that he had an "Old World" education. For example, he would differentiate between "shall" and "will."

Over many years I had an opportunity to learn about Fred's character. He undoubtedly had a close relationship with his mother, an artist, and I think the first graduate of Boston Art School. He had promised her that he would not drink or smoke, and he kept that promise all of his life.

He was a "little fellow," as he described himself. One time my wife, Em, and I visited Fred's beautiful estate on Cotuit Bay. We walked out on the patio overlooking the bay and he said, "Jim, I was a little fellow at Harvard and they took it out on me. I wish that I now had the whole class out there on the lawn in front of us. I would tell them, 'Nyaa, I made it.' But I can't. They're all dead!" He was approaching 100 at the time.

Another time I ran into him outside the Union Club in downtown Cleveland. He had just turned 80 and he told me so. I said, "Fred, don't worry about it, I'll bet your father lived 'til 90." He looked over, bowed to get his head near my ear, and said, "Ninety-four, ninety-four!"

On his 70th birthday I was in his Euclid Avenue office near the TRW plant. He said, "Jim, I'll trade places with you anytime." Finding that difficult to believe (coming from the chairman of TRW), I said, "Fred, why would you want to do that?" He smiled and said, "Youth...Youth...Youth." Many times over the years he said, "I feel like I'm a young man trying to get ahead." I didn't fully understand that at the time, but later on I did.

Many times I walked with him through the TRW plant. His relationship with his employees was heartwarming. He would stop at a lathe and speak to the operator, using the fellow's first name, and ask him about his children by name. There was no doubt that his employee relationships were unique.

Fred and I both happened to be at the Western Reserve Historical Society one day and we spent some time bringing each other up to date. When we finished, a man approached and said, "Fred, I'm one of your machinists and I'd like to get your picture." Fred said okay. But he added, "Your job isn't so great now, is it?" And the fellow said, "No Fred, it isn't." Fred said, "Well I can tell you why -- you fellows voted out the apprentice system and now you're paying the price." And the fellow said, "Fred, you're right, there's too much automation." Then the fellow took out his camera and said, "Fred, I'd like to get your picture." When I stepped away, the man said, "No, no, I want to get you with your friend, Jim." So Fred and I stood there arm in arm and he took our picture. Obviously the employee felt comfortable talking and giving an honest opinion to the chairman of the board of TRW about how he felt about his job.

One Sunday morning at Fred's home, we were meeting in a room in the rear of the house when there was a knock on the front door. Fred said, "Jim, you'll have to excuse me, it's the cook's day off so I'll have to answer the door." He answered the door and I could hear talking. In a few minutes Fred returned and said, "I'm going to be a few minutes longer than I thought; I've got a little problem." He left and there was more talking. Five minutes later he was back in with a smile on his face and said, "That was one of the night watchmen from our plant. I've told our people that if they have a problem to take it to their boss and if it's not solved just keep going up the line until they get to me." This visitor, who was black, had said to Fred that his problem was that TRW "didn't pay him enough." And Fred said, "Well, let me see your budget." And the night watchman was prepared and pulled out his budget and Fred went over it line by line. Fred told me that he came to an item of $2,000 and said, "What's this?" And the night watchman said, "Mr. Crawford, they take it from me." And Fred said, "What do you mean, they take it from you?" And he said, "They just do." So Fred said he made a phone call and found out that the night watchman was buying savings bonds and had $2,000 of savings bonds he didn't know he had. He obviously went away happy.

I never saw Fred angry. In fact one time I asked his secretary, Betty, if Fred ever gets angry, and she said, "Oh yes! He does!" But the only time I ever saw anything that even approached anger was when we were at a meeting and Fred said, "I just saw X" (I forget who it was), but he said, "I just looked right through him!" Another time he agreed to make a solicitation and talked to the head of a smaller Cleveland company. He reported, "When I got through with my little 'asking,' he just said, 'No!'" And that's just the way Fred said it, with a real forceful "No." And I said, "What did you say, Fred?" He said, "I said, 'look X, there are a lot more gracious ways of saying No.'" Generally speaking he didn't seem to have anything negative about him.

The C&O Railroad owned the Greenbriar Resort, and invited Case to bring a group of people down for a conference. I asked various Cleveland corporations to allow us to use their planes and we flew down to the Greenbriar. Fred came along and suggested that we get a golf match together, which we did. On about the third hole Fred said that they had several bowls of fruit in his cottage and he ate too much and he was going to have to stop and find a restroom. He knocked on the door of a beautiful house set back from the third tee and after several moments he came out arm in arm with the owner of the cottage. They were chatting away as if they had been friends all their lives.

Our caddy was a "hillbilly" from around the Greenbriar and Fred immediately engaged him in a conversation. It turned out that the caddy's family had come to this country a long time ago and had lived in the hills nearby ever since. It was fairly interesting to me to see how Fred, whose forebears came over from England, understood the caddy and his background and how quickly they had a real friendly rapport.

The grounds around Fred's Cotuit mansion included sweeping lawns and, in typical Crawford fashion, an 18-hole golf course he had set up. Just as you might expect from Fred, the course had 18 tees but only one green! Kay Crawford, Fred's wife, told me that one of the guests who liked to play golf when she and her husband visited was Supreme Court Justice Sandra Day O'Connor. Apparently, Sandra is a very good athlete and the only one ever to make a hole-in-one on Fred's little course.

Fred did a lot of things in a very unique way. Once when he was in University Hospitals for some minor surgery, the nurses said that he should stay in the hospital and recuperate. Not Fred. He got up, got dressed, and in a firm way said he was leaving, and he did.

Fred told me a story about an award he received in California for being a leading industrialist in the United States. When they introduced him, he said to Kay, "Let's not walk up there like old people shuffling." (He was over 90 at the time.) "Kay and I just strolled up to the stage," and he demonstrated the stroll.

At the Western Reserve Society black tie celebration of Fred's 100th birthday, he was standing at the head of the receiving line looking very handsome in his tux. I greeted him asking, "How's it going, Fred?" He leaned over and whispered in my ear, "Jim, I can't hear a darn thing!" He always had trouble hearing -- but he was so bright, read lips, and could anticipate what people were going to say anyway!

At a 100th birthday affair at Case Western Reserve University about that time, there was a large gathering and Fred, Jim Biggar, chairman of Nestle, and Alan Ford, chairman of the University's board, were the speakers. Each speaker came to the podium and read prepared remarks. When it came to Fred's turn he walked sharply up to the podium and, with no notes at all, gave a rip-roaring speech.

He obviously understood financial matters very well. He told me he had bought his little home in Shaker Heights during the Depression when he didn't have any money. He convinced the bank to give him a three percent loan because he knew they weren't getting any return from any empty house and they could "bet" on him and might get a return. He told me that he never paid the loan off because he could always do much better by using his investment ability.

Another time when I was at his house he introduced me to his cook. When she left the room he said, "Her son was killed in action in the Army and she's going to get a $10,000 memorial check." He added, "I don't know what to do about that because I could say to her, give me that check and I'll invest it for you and maybe in a few years give you back $100,000. But if I do that, I'll lose a good cook!"

I don't know how wealthy Fred was, but he once sat down with me and wrote on a sheet of paper how much he was investing in tax-free bonds. I got the feeling that he was trying to share his expertise with me. He was a natural teacher. Another time when we were walking out to his corporate plane to take a flight to Detroit to help the Detroit Institute of Technology, he said, "This is the only thing that you don't have that I have." And I said, "What is that, Fred?" And he said, "The corporate planes. I intend to keep control of them as long as I can."

While flying up to Detroit that day, he said that earlier he had run one of the Thompson plants in the Detroit area and that he noticed out his office window trucks coming by with very nice looking sheets of metal that obviously had been cut from bigger sheets. He said, "I knew that they were on their way to a scrap dump, and I thought that was a shame. I investigated and found that I could buy them very cheaply. That's how I started Crawford Door, using those sheets of scrap metal." Many years later he sold Crawford Door to Armstrong Flooring Company. And my recollection was that he got a number of millions -- about $9 million. He was a shrewd businessman, undoubtedly.

One day he told me that he had bought a "little place" up on Cape Cod, and I happened to be talking to his secretary, Betty Thomas, and I said, "I understand that Fred has bought a "little place" on Cape Cod." And she said, "Little place! You ask him about that again!" I saw him later and I said, "Fred, Betty told me that that little place up at Cape Cod isn't so little." And he leaned over and in his New England accent said, "Fourteen bedrooms and fourteen baths." Later he told me how he got the place, which was a beautiful property including a mansion on Cotuit Bay. He said it was in an estate which was sitting there because the owner had died and it was ultimately to go to a young boy who at that time was only seven or eight. Fred said that there was a smaller house up on the edge of the property which he sold for enough to pay for the entire estate.

We visited him and his lovely wife, Kay, at the Cape several times. On the second floor there was a large hallway lined with his mother's paintings which were very beautiful. Since my wife, Em, is an artist, he delighted in showing her those paintings. Later he had one painting a year duplicated for his Christmas cards.

He didn't paint himself but he often drew little pictures of stick men and sent them with his correspondence. I have several of them in my files. When we gave him a small Tupelo or Pepperidge Tree (which I grew as a hobby) when he married Kay, he flew it up to Cape Cod in the company plane and sent me a thank you with a stick-man drawing of the "planting ceremony." When we visited, he would take us out to show us the Tupelo. It didn't grow into a single Tupelo tree but into a bush which turned a very beautiful burgundy in the fall.

Fred played the cello when he was younger and when he heard that I had played the bass fiddle in high school and used it to make money in order to go to college, he told me about his long interest in the cello. Then in typical Fred fashion he said that he had to give it up when he went to TRW because he "couldn't get it into an upper berth!"

Another example of unique abilities was an incident that he told me about. He said TRW had some litigation problems with a company in New England and when it went on for a quite a long time he proposed that the two companies get all their lawyers together in one place. (I think the place where they met was in Vermont.) Fred said that when they got together there were a couple of dozen lawyers ready to do battle. He said he called the chairman of the opposing corporation over to one side and said, "Look, I knew your father and your mother and your family, and this is costing us a lot of money. Why don't we just tell all these lawyers to go home and the two of us can settle it right here?" Which they proceeded to do.

He would often ask me rhetorical questions in good fun. One time when I was at his home in Shaker, he said, "Jim, we've developed a catalytic converter at TRW." That was a great need at that time because auto pollution was a big subject in the country. He added, "It will cost us $125 to produce. My question of you is should we start to produce it and sell it?" And I said, "Fred, there's obviously some twist to this, so why don't you tell me the answer." And he said, "Well, there's no way that you'd be able to add $125 to every car and get the people to pay for it. Even though there's a great need out in California, and other places, the only way that this is going to be done is if they pass a law saying that all cars should have a catalytic converter. In that case we could make them and sell them but otherwise for the time-being there's no way to do that."

I would often ask him a question and say, "Tell me in one sentence what you think." When he went to China at a time when not many people were going to China, I said, "Fred, tell me in one sentence what you think of China." He was very quick with the answer. He said, "If they ever discover the free enterprise system, they'll drive us off the face of the earth." Another time I said, "Fred, what do you think is wrong with the country?" when there were a lot of unusual things happening during the 60's. In one word he said, "Affluence."

Another time when I was at his house, he got a card table and said he was going to show me one of the great naval battles in the Virgin Islands when a new method of naval warfare was developed. He put out a number of small checkers representing the British Navy and the opposing navy ships. He said that rather than facing the other ships as apparently they did at that time, the British went in an alignment where they would be able to face the ships at first but also be able to turn the ships at a ninety degree angle that brought the line into a different configuration with the enemy and allowed them to move between the opposing ships and win the battle decisively.

I think he would have made a great history professor.

When Fred retired from TRW, he turned over the reins to his friend, Dave Wright, who was a tax professor at Western Reserve University before he went to TRW. Fred had great respect for Dave Wright and explained how he chose him. He said, "There were three very good contenders for the presidency. One was Dave Wright, the second one was Lee Clegg, and the third was Arch Colwell," all good men. "I had to figure out some way that would make them feel good about it because I obviously could choose only one. I waited until it was time to pass out their salary letters for the next year and I asked them to come in to my office together. I gave the first salary letter to Arch Colwell. It was for $75,000, and I showed it to all of them. Then I gave the second one to Lee, and that also was for $75,000. And then I gave the final one to Dave, and it was for $75,000.01!"

We often traded stories and jokes. He had a great sense of humor. He would relate stories from the past that I found very interesting. One time he told me about how he had an order from Henry Ford for a certain automobile part that TRW made, but Ford specified that the part should be sent in a box of very specific dimensions which had to be put together on the corners with tongue and groove. Fred said that he knew that Henry Ford was a very shrewd businessman, so he kept thinking about the order until he came up with the answer. Ford was using the top and bottom of the boxes as the floorboards for the Model T.

    Fred had many friends because people just liked to be around him. I once asked him, "Who was the most gracious man you ever met?" And he said, "Without a doubt, Winston Churchill." He said, "Churchill could walk into a room of 17 people and put them at ease faster than any man I ever saw." So could Fred. He also told me that he had met Nehru and had asked Nehru what was the greatest problem in India. Nehru had quickly answered, "Population growth." And he said that birth control was the answer, but he didn't know if he would be able to sell that to the Indian people. He also told me that he had met with the head of the Fiat automobile conglomerate in Italy and that Mr. Fiat had asked him how to continue to make a profit when the price producing cars was continually inflating. Fred said, "I told him it was a very simple procedure. You just pay your people enough so that they can buy the cars." And he meant it. He used to write notes to me addressed to "banker" because he realized that I was doing very well, and of course he was too. He once came into my office at Case and plunked 1,000 shares of TRW on my desk and said, "That's a gift to Case and don't even thank me for it because I think my base cost of each one of those shares of stock is about one cent." The stock at that time was $83. I watched it for awhile and I don't think it topped $83 (at least that I remember), for quite some time. He obviously knew what he was doing.

    He said many times that Cleveland should have had most of the big airplane corporations that were spread all over the country because most of the top people who founded those corporations, including Martin, Douglas & McDonnell, had been in Cleveland and left because they couldn't get the financing that they needed from the Cleveland banks. They went where they could get the financing.

He was quick to support any idea that was unusual and perhaps risky. At a trustee meeting over at the Wade Park Manor I proposed that our objective at Case should be to make Case the kind of institution in the Midwest that California Institute of Technology and Massachusetts Institute of Technology were on the East and West Coasts. He picked that up like a "pot of gold" and used it thereafter.

Edgar Hahn was the founder of one of the major legal firms in Cleveland, and early in my career at Case Institute, I had the opportunity to spend some time with Mr. Hahn. He knew that I had quite a great deal of affection for Fred Crawford and told me that he too thought that Fred was very unique and he said that he had an opportunity to affect Fred's early career in Cleveland. Apparently, when it came time to choose who should lead TRW, the New York group who controlled TRW financially asked Edgar Hahn to recommend someone who should take over the firm. Edgar Hahn said that when he looked into the matter there was no doubt in his mind that Fred was very unusual and was the man for the job. He said he went back to New York and convinced the financial people to support Fred and he was very proud to tell me he had made the right decision. Almost all people that Fred touched seemed to be of the same opinion.

When I found out that the Olin Foundation of Minneapolis was giving entire buildings to colleges and universities, I learned that Charles Horn ran the foundation. I mentioned this to Fred and he said, "Oh I know Charlie Horn, we correspond regularly. He writes me letters complaining that I'm not getting enough return on the assets of TRW." And I said, "Do you think you could get an appointment to see him?" And he said, "Well, I'm not sure but I could certainly give it a try."

When it came time to choose someone to lead his sizeable foundation after his death, Mr. Olin didn't name any of his children or any of his associates, but rather he named Charlie Horn who headed one of his competitors. In due course, we made a proposal to Charlie Horn for a building. Almost everybody at Case said it wouldn't succeed because the Olin Foundation required that the building be completely separate and free-standing and Case was short of land. I suggested that we build it next to one of the other buildings at Case and that we put a glass passageway between the two. We tried that out with Charlie Horn, and it worked.

When Charlie Horn came to Cleveland for the dedication of the Olin Building, we were walking across the campus and stopped at the old administration building, Charlie Horn said, "You ought to do something about this old building." And I said, "Well, why don't you do something in honor of Fred." And he said, "I might do that." Ultimately we got another building from him and named it the Crawford Building.

An interesting sidelight in connection with the Crawford Building is that Bill Hargett of Hargett and Hoag, who were engineering-architects, said it was too bad that Case was going outside Cleveland for much of its architecture and that he had a gift which he wanted to show to me. It was an architectural rendering of the Crawford Building almost exactly as it exists today. When we made a proposal to Olin for the Crawford Building, we just pulled out Hargett's depiction and it won the day.

Charles Spahr, the chairman of Sohio, said many times that when it came time for him to decide how Sohio was going to deal with its unions, he talked to Fred and found out how Fred had developed his association with the unions (which is a story that I'm sure can be better told by others). He used Fred's philosophy and methods of approach and they worked beautifully for Standard Oil of Ohio.

Many times when I would be in the Union Club at lunchtime I would run into Dave Ford who was one of the wealthiest men in Cleveland. He always wanted to talk about Fred and he would ask me to bring him up to date on what Fred was doing and how he was doing. The same was true of Roger Clapp, who became chairman of Lubrizol and was one of Cleveland's major philanthropists, along with his wife, Ann. Anytime Roger was in a party where I was, the chief subject of conversation between the two of us, was

James C. Hardie

Fred Crawford. Tom Lord, chairman of Lord Corporation, in Erie, Pennsylvania, became associated with Case Institute because Tom had been at Yale at the same time as Keith Glennan and the Lord Corporation president, Don Alstadt, was a graduate student at the University of Pittsburgh about the time that I graduated. A good example of the way we worked closely with those corporations who were members of the Case Associates is exemplified by our work with the Lord Corporation in Erie. Alstadt, who was a brilliant researcher with more than 50 patents, told me that often times at different Lord plants around the country, they were duplicating work and design done in other areas because they had no good way to document what had been done and where it had been done. I thought about that for awhile and decided to talk to our computer people who at that time were in the forefront of computing in the country. I learned that it was possible to use the telephone lines to transmit data and I asked one of our star faculty members, Dr. Fred Way, if data could be sent from Erie over the telephone lines to Case, and he said yes.

Subsequently, I went down to Erie and talked to Don Alstadt about the problem and we drew up a simple contract that specified a method of transferring their designs and other important information into a database and work out a way of retrieving this data when the Lord Corporation wanted to do so. Specifically, what this enabled the Lord Corporation to do, for example, was allow an engineer in Pennsylvania who was designing a new piece of equipment relative to "coatings" to search the database and find out if that same piece of equipment had been designed before by somebody else.

In today's computer atmosphere, this seems to be almost ridiculously simple but there were two things in this project that were breakthroughs: 1) the use of the database in that way, and 2) transmitting the information over telephone lines.

Incidentally, I think we agreed that Lord should pay Case $1000 for this development.

Lord and Alstadt attended all of the meetings for the Case Associates because of Fred. He was the star that attracted all the satellites. Then I introduced Tom Lord to the Cleveland Clinic at his request and got my doctor, Victor DeWolfe, to be Tom's doctor at the Clinic. Later on, Tom gave many millions of dollars to the Cleveland Clinic, because he said Vic was the only doctor who always told him the truth.

Fred was always optimistic and positive, and "young." He said to me that when you get old you get cynical and "the Lord takes you off the face of the earth."

While I was still vice president of Case, Fred asked me to do a special public relations job with the Auto Museum when it was on Chester Avenue. He said there was a problem concerning Mrs. Sumerladd, who was the director of what was then called the Crawford Auto Museum. He said that Mrs. Sumerladd was retiring and was unhappy with what was happening and asked me if I could straighten it out. When I met Mrs. Sumerladd, it was evident to me that she was unhappy with the fact that they seemed to be letting her go off into oblivion without recognizing how much she had meant to the Auto Museum. So I said, "Mrs. Sumerladd, I know you probably don't want it, but I think we really ought to make your retirement an important affair for the Auto Museum and I'm going to make a suggestion to Fred that we have a nice dinner to thank you for all your accomplishments. I could see that this pleased her so I went back to the office and wrote a story about a fictitious press conference which was supposedly held in connection with Mrs. Sumerladd's retirement. I don't think you could do that today. It was a totally fictitious story but I wrote it and the papers were nice enough to accept it. After writing about Mrs. Sumerladd's retirement, I said that there were several questions from the reporters who attended this fictitious press conference, and one of the questions was, "Mr. Crawford, how would you describe Mrs. Sumerladd's connection with the Auto Museum?" And I wrote that Fred answered that, "She was the engine behind the Auto Museum." Then I said that the reporter asked, "Well, if she was the engine behind the Auto Museum, Mr. Crawford, what were you?" And I said that Fred answered, "Just say that I was the squirrel's tail on the radiator ornament." Later when the story was published in the paper, I talked to Fred's secretary, Betty Thomas, and said, "What did Fred think of the story?" And she said that he looked at it and chuckled and then said, "That gawdam Jim!"

I know the year was 1972 because I have in my office a framed award signed by both Fred and Meredith Colkett commemorating my service to the Western Reserve Historical Society.

Fred told me how he came to start his little Auto Museum, and he said it was because one of his old acquaintances asked him for a thousand dollars and Fred told him he would give him a thousand dollars but he was afraid he would lose a friend. So he said to the friend, "Do you have anything at all that I could buy for a thousand dollars?" And the fellow said that he had an old car in a barn (I forget where) and that he could sell that old car to Fred for a thousand dollars. Fred said that when restored, that car became the first automobile in the Crawford Auto Museum.

Another time when I was having lunch with Wade Harris he asked me what happened to the company that Fred Crawford started which grew quickly and ended up on the big board? (I'll have to research what the company was named but I think it was something like "Boron" but I'm not sure of that.) The company was composed of a group of consultants who would provide consulting to cracking plants in the oil industry.

I answered, "Wade, I talked this over with Fred Crawford and as you probably know the company has gone out of business. Fred explained that the idea was a sound one but what he didn't foresee was that IBM had cornered many of the people who could do the work that Boron required so they went out of business because they couldn't get the necessary personnel."

Wade, who was very bright, and certainly was a friend, or at least admired Fred Crawford, said, "Jim, if your friend Fred Crawford is so great, why didn't he anticipate that the company wouldn't be able to garner the proper people to be employees?"

I guess nobody's perfect!

Later when I left Case to be a consultant, Fred asked me to become a consultant to the Western Reserve Historical Society and said that the Society was endeavoring to raise a substantial amount of money to build a library and that the campaign was stuck. He asked me to resurrect the campaign and make it successful. They needed a development officer and he felt that a young man who was connected with the Society by the name of Dave Twining might be a director of development, and asked me to train him. Fred called him "General Twining." Twining worked out very well as a director of development and I think he is now a history professor at one of the colleges in Pennsylvania. We put together a first-rate campaign steering committee which included Fred, Scott Mueller, Paul Walter, David Ingalls, Dave Swetland, John Tormey and John Baird. John was a good friend and, I suppose you could say, "best friend" of Alex Nason, who had been chairman of Lubrizol. When we got to a point where we wanted to put a proposal to support the library before the Nason Foundation, John was very helpful. Alex Nason came to town and said he wanted to meet with Fred and myself at the Mayfield Country Club where he was a prominent member. We went out to have lunch with him and he announced that he wanted to tell both Fred and me about his decision personally, and that the Nason Foundation was going to give the Historical Society a million dollars, ostensibly in our honor.

Also, Fred said to me that he felt that young David Ingalls, the son of David Ingalls, Sr., who had been the first naval ace, would be a good man for the steering committee at the Society, and we subsequently asked Dave. This began my long relationship with David Ingalls, who became a key person, not only for the Society but for two other institutions with which I consulted -- The Museum of Natural History, and Hawken School.

After Twining left to teach, I arranged for another director of development for the Society, a young lady by the name of Kathy Culley, and we worked very hard to develop annual giving at the Society which always seemed to be short of operating funds. One of the key people in connection with these efforts was Trustee John Tormey, who was on the board of the GAR Foundation in Akron, which was named for Galen and Ruth Roush. Roush was a graduate of Case Western Reserve Law School. (Of interest relative to Roush, is that when I became vice president of both Case Western Reserve and Case, I went over to talk with the president of Western Reserve,

Jack Millis, and in the midst of the conversation I said I'm sure glad to inherit the interest of one of the wealthiest men in northeastern Ohio, the graduate of your law school, Galen Roush, and he said, "Jim, I've never heard of Galen Roush." Which emphasizes the importance of having a development office that does some research.)

Even though the Knight Foundation didn't then make gifts in Cleveland, Jack Knight, a Pulitzer Prize winner, married Clevelander Mrs. Albert Augustus, and at Fred's request, made a major gift to the Society.

Once when we were up at Cape Cod having dinner with Fred and Kay at the mansion, Fred said, "Jim, last Friday, David Packard was here for dinner and he was sitting in the chair you are sitting in and that day David made $3 million because of an upswing in the stock of Hewlett Packard. How much did you make?" And I said, "Fred, I'm going to change chairs."

Fred's father was a lawyer and he didn't talk much about his father. Most everything was about his mother. But I do remember he told me a story about his father sitting at the kitchen table counting some money he had made at a time when they needed the money. Suddenly a gust of wind came through the house and blew the money out the window. I wish I could say that they rushed out and gathered up all the money but I'm sorry I don't know any more about the story than that, but I do know that the inference was that it was needed at that time -- sort of a Murphy's Law.

In the 70's, Fred told me that he had met every president of the United States alive in Fred's lifetime. He had a family relationship with President Coolidge, but I'll leave that to others more knowledgeable to comment on. He said that there is no comparison with sitting across the desk from the President of the United States when he asked you to do something for your country. He said you might go in expecting to say no, but when you get there in that position, something happens to you, and you say yes.

Tom Lester is one of the major donors to the Western Reserve Historical Society. Tom became a member of the Western Reserve Historical Society board because of his great respect for Fred Crawford. Tom said that his success in founding his little company was due to Fred Crawford's help. Ultimately, Tom gave the Society thousands of dollars in honor of Fred.

Fred had some interesting comments about the British. He said that it was very difficult to do business with the British because of their early history with smuggling due to their unique geographical position. He said that smuggling caused all sorts of problems between the smugglers and the British who were receiving the smuggled items. However, he added that you could give one of your English friends a thousand dollars and ask him to keep it for you and that you would pick it up when you saw him in Paris. Even if you didn't see him until months later, you could be absolutely assured that he would have the thousand dollars for you.

One of the wonderful organizations which Fred started (I had nothing to do with it) was Blue Coats, the well-known organization which provides for the families of policemen who are killed in the line of duty. Fred not only started the organization, but personally enlisted most of the members of Blue Coats.

When a Cleveland corporate leader accepted a position of importance in a philanthropic effort all of the remaining corporate leaders came together to make sure that his effort was successful, especially if he had not taken that kind of leadership in the past. I feel that this was one of the important legacies of Fred Crawford. Of course, some people never stepped up to a leadership position in part, I think, because they feared failure and partially because they could always say that they were too busy, which I'm sure they were. Sometimes, I think it was because they were not substantial donors and it takes years of giving into the great pot of philanthropic needs before you begin to earn the right to take some of that money back by asking others to give. I remember that sometime along the way when Fred Crawford was doing his yeomen work in philanthropic leadership, he said to me that when he was a successful young executive, he didn't give away nearly enough and it was only after he started to make substantial gifts later in his career that he learned that "When he did so, he never missed the money that he gave."

I'm sure that many studies have been made about the importance of giving which have delved into the psychological

James C. Hardie

background of the entire philanthropic tradition. But one thing that I'm certain of is that some areas of the country, like Cleveland, developed a philanthropic tradition and many others never got started philanthropically because they didn't have a "Fred Crawford." I remember a conversation I had with Fred Ball, the chairman of the Ball Company in Muncie, Indiana, and he was talking to me about being a consultant to raise money for the Ball Memorial Hospital. I noted in talking to him that most of the institutions in Muncie at that time, like the YMCA and the hospital, had been given to the community by the Ball company. As I explained to him where the money for the expansion of the Ball Memorial Hospital might come from, I mentioned that the employees of the Ball Company and other major corporations would give substantially. He said to me, "I just find that so difficult to understand, Jim. Do you really mean that the employees of our company would make gifts for something like the hospital?" And I said, "Yes, they're doing it in other parts of the country. All you have to do is get a leadership group together and ask them. While they won't make gifts such as the hundreds of thousands that your company has given, when you take a thousand employees and get them to give an average of $80 each, it adds up to a substantial gift." He shook his head in disbelief. And when we did the campaign, we were very successful and I'm certain that just getting started on that kind of giving from employees and others in Muncie, Indiana, has served them well in the interim. I'm also fairly certain that that type of giving would not have come about if it were not for the leadership of Fred Crawford and TRW in setting a pattern of giving for others to follow.

One of Fred's best friends in Cleveland was Gordon Stouffer, and the only picture I remember in the living room of the Shaker house was a picture of Gordon Stouffer. As a result of that friendship, Fred was very important to the Stouffer Corporation. While he was not on the board, he was considered a very important advisor, and I remember that when the Litton Corporation made a presentation to Vernon Stouffer to buy Stouffers, Gordon's brother, Fred, (Gordon had died earlier) told me he advised Vernon to turn down the offer. He said he told Vernon that he had a nice little family company there, and "you've got control of it -- why don't you turn it down?" Which Vernon did, but later Fred said they got Vernon on a fishing expedition somewhere in the Bahamas and talked him into selling the company. Fred said, "Jim, they can do this because of the inflation going on right now but you just watch." And he cocked the end of his finger down, "They'll be a downturn and there's going to be a big loss as far as Stouffer is concerned." And that's the way it happened.

When Fred was speaking before a group he liked to see their faces and talk directly to them even if it was a large group.

One time when we were having a campaign kickoff before several hundred people in one of the Cleveland auditoriums, we were using a large mock-up of the Case campus, and Fred was moving mock-ups of the various buildings around to show how the campus would change. But at the time, one of my staff members, Eldon Winkler, who was an expert in theater lighting, was manipulating the lights in order to spotlight the large model of the campus. But when the lights were dimmed, Fred couldn't see the faces of the audience and he quickly got word back to me and I told Eldon to forget about the theatrical effects and turn up the lights.

Although Fred was a slight man in his declining years, I've seen pictures of him as a young man and he was rather muscular. I know that he worked at keeping in shape.

He told me that he "skinny-dipped" (swam in the nude) off the point of their property when he was at his place at Cat Cay in the Bahamas. He also told me that in Cleveland each time he came down the stairs in the morning, there was a place that he could hang from, which is a very good exercise, and he did that every day. Also, toward the end of his life when he was in Cleveland at his Bratenahl apartment, he would walk every night a certain number of steps. He had great posture and one time when we drove together from the Cleveland Airport, and I dropped him off at his Shaker home, we talked about posture. Fred had great posture, and I didn't.

Fred also knew Jimmy Doolittle and indicated many times that he thought that Doolittle was the greatest living hero at that time in the United States.

John Sherwin, Sr., then chairman of the Western Reserve University board, and I saw him on Euclid Avenue and we walked along together and he said, "Jim, every time I look at what Case is doing, you fellows are three or four steps ahead of us and every time we catch up you seem to jump ahead. Why is that?" And I said, "Well, John, in my opinion, it's because of a lot of things but most of all because of Fred Crawford." And I still think that is true.

It's interesting to note that for much of the time, Fred was out of town. He spent substantial time at his place at Cat Cay in the Bahamas and some time each year in Vermont and at the mansion on Cape Cod. We would schedule numerous events around the comparably few dates when he was back in Cleveland, which gave the impression that he was in town more than he was. When Fred came to town, important things happened!

Fred's burial plot is in Lakeview Cemetery under a big oak tree. By a sheer happenstance, the Hardie plot in Lakeview Cemetery is next to Fred's. When I found that out, I told Fred that we could trade jokes underground and share happy memories.

Like Abu Ben Adam, Fred "loved his fellow man" and his tribe increased.

One of the most important members of his philanthropic tribe was Charlie White.

Since Charlie ran the biggest employer in the Cleveland area, Republic Steel, he had enormous influence. When we were getting ready to conduct the $6 million campaign shortly after I arrived at Case, we were in the philanthropic era that called for two-thirds of a major campaign to be given by corporations. Also, we were still using the format of a chairman at the top of the campaign and a corporate chairman and a special gifts chairman immediately under him. I said, "Fred, we need Charlie White to be Corporate Chairman." Fred said, "Jim, go get Hassel Tippit," who was chairman of the Case development committee, and get Tip to come over and ask me to be campaign chairman. We were then at a cocktail party at Case in advance of an affair which escapes me. But I got Tip and clued him in and we strolled over to where Fred was talking to Charlie White. Tip said, "Fred, as you know we're going to conduct a $6 million campaign and I hope that you'll agree to be chairman." And Fred said, "Well, you know that's a big job and I've got a lot to do. I don't know if I can do that." And Charlie White being a great guy and a wonderful supporter said, "Ah, Fred, I think you're the only man who can do it and I think you ought to do it." And Fred said, "Well, maybe you're right, Charlie, but I'll do it if you agree to be corporate chairman." There was no way that Charlie was going to say no!

As things developed, I had a very enjoyable and successful relationship with Charlie White. A lot of people thought he was less than a smart guy but in my opinion he had tremendous abilities and at six feet five he towered over everybody and was so darn honest and different and humourous that he became a great asset to me and to Case.

One time when I was in his office at the time that Richard Nixon was running for President, Charlie called Tom Watson at IBM and told me to stay. Charlie was a great Republican and was raising a lot of money for the Republican Party. When he got Tom Watson on the phone he said, "Tom, I need another $10,000." There was silence for about thirty seconds and Charlie very slowly hung up the phone and said, "Jim, you'll never believe what he said. He said he couldn't do it because he's for Kennedy." Then he picked up the phone and called somewhere in Republic and he said, "Get all those damn IBM computers and stuff out of the company." Two minutes passed and the phone rang again and Charlie took it and he then put the phone down again and he said, "Jim, they say they can't do it."

Republic had a small executive dining room on the twentieth floor overlooking the "flats" where Republic Steel had some plants. Once when I was having lunch with Charlie (just the two of us), he walked over to the window overlooking the flats and said to me, "Jim, you see that smoke coming up there? They call it 'pollution.' I suppose it is, but to me it will always be a pleasant sight because it means my people are working." Often I would go to his office and he would be sitting there in front of an absolutely clean desk and he would say, "What do you want me to do?" And I would say, "Charlie, I have some things which I hope you will do." I would list them, and he would think a moment and say, "I'll have them done before the day is out because I would like to get out of here and go home to play with my granddaughter." One time I said, "Charlie, I've asked you to do many things many times and you've always agreed. Why do you do it?" And he thought awhile and said, "I guess I think that if I don't do it, it won't get done."

Another time I wanted to get down to Youngstown to visit with Ed Thomas and Charlie agreed to get an appointment and go down with me. He said he would have his limousine pick me up so we could go down together. On the way down he said to me, "Jim, you know that I became chairman of Republic after my friend, Tom Girdler, was pushed out as chairman, and I'd like to tell you about that because most people think that I used devious methods to get rid of Tom." He then proceeded to tell me the story. It ended up that he said that both he and Tom went to a board meeting which was rather contentious and various board members started asking questions and Charlie said, "I answered each question as honestly as I could. And when we got through I was very surprised to be named chairman."

You just couldn't help but like the guy. I remember he said to me, "Jim, do you know where the loneliest place is in the country on Christmas Eve?" And I said, "No Charlie." And he said, "On top of a blast furnace." The implication was that as he was going up the line at Republic he became Chief Engineer, and if something went wrong, the chief engineer was called out and he had to respond, even on Christmas Eve. That comment stayed with me when Fred Crawford said to me, "Jim, you know I don't have any children and that makes Christmas Eve a very lonely time."

I should say what happened at the meeting with Ed Thomas, who now has a very lovely Memorial Auditorium built in his honor in Akron: Taking out the pleasantries, the result of the meeting was that Ed Thomas said, "Charlie, you run Cleveland -- I'll run Akron."

When Russian Premier Khrushchev came to this country, a small number of prominent industrialists, including Charlie, were invited to Washington, D. C. to meet with him. Charlie, who had no love of Russia or the communists, was always having trouble with Gus Hall, the head of the Communist Party in Ohio. Charlie told me that they arranged about 25 chairs for the industrialists and Khrushchev sat on one chair facing them and he was rather rotund and he overlapped the sides of the chair. When Khrushchev got through speaking he asked if anybody had any questions. Charlie said, "Well, you know, I'm six foot five so I stood up and there was no doubt that he could see me and I said, 'Mr. Khrushchev, why is it that every time we have some problem in Ohio and trace it back we find that your man, Gus Hall, who is head of the Communist Party in Ohio, is behind it? What are you going to do about it?'" He said Khrushchev started to laugh, and he laughed so hard that Charlie thought he was going to fall off the chair. And when he composed himself he said, "Mr. White, if you ever send any Gus Halls to Russia we won't ask you to do anything about it, <u>we'll</u> take care of it!" And Charlie said, "I couldn't blame him. I think he was right."

Another time we were having a breakfast meeting and he came in and said that his wife, who he loved dearly, had dragged him to the opera the night before. And I said, "Charlie, which opera was it?" And he said, "Jim, when you get past God Bless America, I'm lost, I don't know."

Charlie was always at odds with the unions and they had some pretty violent strikes at Republic Steel. I wasn't an observer of the following story but I'm sure it is a true one. The union was striking one of the plants in Youngstown and Charlie went down with a group of executives to keep the plant running while the strike was on. The story is that they decided to go through the union line in order to get into the plant, and there was a little violence, but they made it. Later on there was a trial and Charlie was forced to testify. When he did, they asked him what had happened and Charlie said, "Well, we wanted to get into the plant and we walked through the line and went into the plant." And they asked if there was a fight. And Charlie said, "Oh, maybe as far as my own recollection goes I brushed against somebody." And a big guy stood up in the back of the courtroom and hollered, "Brushed against me, hell, he broke my arm!"

James C. Hardie

Once when we were having a big meeting (I think it was one of the Michelson Award dinners referenced later in this book) for a large number of people at the Case gym, we had a board meeting before the affair which Charlie White attended. When it came time to go over to the gym for the meeting, Charlie said, "Jim, do I have to go over to that meeting? There's nothing I'd rather do than go home and play with my granddaughter." And I said, "Charlie, there are going to be about 600 people over there who feel the same way as you. But they'll look up at the head table and you're bigger than everybody else so they'll see you and say if Charlie White can take the time to attend, I guess I can too." Charlie said, "Gawdamit, let's go!" As we walked over to the gym, President Glennon said, "Jim, I wouldn't have had the guts to say that!"

Charlie and his beloved wife, Mary, were best friends of Lester and Ruth Sears. Lester Sears was a consummate engineer. He invented the lift truck and founded Towmotor and ultimately merged Towmotor into Caterpillar. Lester and Ruth's daughter, Maryann, was a lovely woman who was married to David Swetland. She was David's first wife. The Case campus was made up of only 32 acres and Lester would talk to me often about how we could rearrange the entrance and egress to make the campus more efficient. Later I think I made one of my best contributions by suggesting that we build buildings along what then was called Chester Avenue so that we had a designed wall of buildings on that side overhanging the hillside, which would allow us to pick up a great amount of space. That carried the day and worked out very well. We asked Lester and Ruth to give us a new library which would be part of that "wall," and they agreed to make a gift of a million dollars.

I went to West Palm Beach, Florida, where the Sears and Whites had side-by-side condos, to pick up the million dollars. It was a very enjoyable trip. I particularly remember that Maryann, the Sears' daughter, was especially gracious. Lester was not well and showed me a little tin where he had some pills and he said, "That pill is my pancreas. And the other pill is something else, etc." He was still bright and articulate. He had two boats there, both of them about 125 feet long; one of them which he was trying to sell, and the other one was new. He took me out on a trip around the West Palm Beach waterways. Ruth, his wife, who was a plain spoken, dogmatic person, sat in the back in a beautiful designed area of the yacht, a rotunda where you could look out and see in all directions. And I said, "Ruth, this is pretty nice." And she said, "Jim, this is not my style, I'm not interested in this, it's too ostentatious." She outlived Lester by many years and set up the Sears Foundation and I had a number of dealings with her in connection with various clients where she had a keen interest. I remember once when she was attending a special luncheon in connection with Wade Park Manor, I waited to squire her into the meeting for the luncheon. On the way into the luncheon as we were walking down the hallway I was making small talk and she leaned over closer to me and said, "Get me a man!"

As we rode around on the boat trip, Lester pointed out some of the beautiful land owned by a few of the old families of Cleveland and he noted that they didn't sell because it was a tremendous legacy. The land kept going up with inflation; probably faster than inflation.

When the Sears Library was built, the lobby was dedicated to one of the grand ladies of Cleveland, Louise Ireland, and the front area, which included the reference room, was dedicated to George Dively's Harris Corporation.

When we got around to dedicating the library, we put together a small dinner party for Lester and Ruth Sears and I talked to Professor Harry Mergler, who was on the cutting edge of research in computers and asked him if he could come up with something that would appeal to Lester Sears. Harry said, "What is he interested in?" And I told him about the new boat. And he said, "Maybe I can make him a digital odometer." And I said, "Harry, what's a digital odometer?" And he said, "Well, if you remember in the old days of sailing vessels, in order to figure out their actual speed because the current impacts the speed of the vessel, they used to have a log on a rope and toss it off of the back and then compute the actual speed relative to the current that way. I think I can come up with a little computer that does that automatically." I said, "I think that's a great idea." And he built the computer.

At the dinner we explained to Lester that we were giving him this gift and it was a digital odometer and explained quickly how it worked. He was an engineer and could see the advantages of the odometer immediately. When we took a picture of the presentation of the odometer, I said to him, "Lester, put your hand on the odometer." And he said, "Jim, I can't keep my hands off of it."

Later, Ruth told me that he went down to their place in Florida and, for the first time in years, took out his old engineering overalls and installed the odometer which had a thin tube that went around the hull of the boat and up to the deck. She said he wouldn't let anybody else touch it -- that he installed it entirely himself. This was also my introduction to David Swetland, and in due course the Sears Foundation became the Sears Swetland Family Foundation, which started a long and pleasant association for me with David Swetland. But in those early days, Ruth didn't like any interference from David, so asking for money for the Sears Foundation became a touchy situation.

An addenda on the digital odometer: Jim Hodge, was the chairman of Warner and Swazey, which was a fine Cleveland company at that time. Hodge had graduated from Case. He and Elmer Lindseth graduated from Case in the 20's, one from John Hay and the other from (I think) Glenville High School, and they both got scholarships to Case. Parenthetically, I think Elmer told me that John Hay or Glenville at that time had more Ph.D. teachers than Case.

Jim Hodge was a Scotsman who came over from Scotland when he was ten and profited from the wonderful education that he received in Scotland before he came here. Hodge called me and said that he would like to talk to Harry Mergler about his digital odometer. So I worked out an arrangement for them to meet and Hodge offered Mergler $600,000 for the idea, and Harry agreed. Later, when Hodge delivered the check for $600,000 to Harry, it was coming on a weekend, and Hodge called me and said, "What's your friend going to do with the check?" And I said, "I don't know." "Well," he said, "If I have any understanding of human beings, I think that he probably took it home to show to his family and the weekend is coming up, but that isn't a wise thing to do. I think you should call him and tell him to run that check right down to the bank so he can start getting interest on it immediately," which I did. In short order, Harry bought a schooner with part of his money. He was not a sailor, but he entered a race on Lake Erie and, using his digital odometer, won it.

Hodge became a great friend and, not only did he take leadership with Case, but he was also interested in the Salvation Army when I became a consultant to them. David Swetland became a key person in many of my future clients including the Western Reserve Historical Society, Western Reserve Academy in Hudson, and the Garden Center (now the Cleveland Botanical Gardens). His daughter, Ruth Eppig, has also become a leader in philanthropy in Cleveland.

I have mentioned before that Charlie White was a diehard Republican and after Eisenhower was elected president and a few weeks had passed, I saw Charlie and asked him how he thought Eisenhower was doing. Eisenhower, being a life-long military man, had no experience in the political arena. Charlie said, "Jim, Ike is in about the same position that I would be if someone asked me to say mass in a Catholic church. I'd take the incense from the altar boys at the wrong time or I'd turn to the wrong page in the Bible or genuflect at the wrong time and I'd be so dependent on the altar boys that they might give me the wrong thing at the wrong time."

But, he said, "He'll learn fast, and I'm sure he'll be a great president."

One day when we were having a meeting of the trustees at the Union Club, most of those who were supposed to attend were already sitting around the table when Wade Harris, a trustee of Case and chairman of Midland Ross, literally burst into the room and rather red-faced sat down and said, "I think it's just terrible that all of us here who are members of the Union Club are not paying for our membership out of personal funds but rather out of our corporate funds."

He was really concerned about this and after some further comments along the same lines he said, "Okay, I'll ask you. How

James C. Hardie

many in this room pay for your own membership in the Union Club?" He had opened up a rather volatile subject and I could see that the group sitting around the table was embarrassed, until Charlie White, who had a marvelous ability to lead (which I think few people recognized), slowly raised his hand in answer to the question and said, "I don't!" That diffused the whole problem.

One day Charlie White called me and said, "Jim, we're having trouble getting our record of Republic Steel gifts straight, and I hope that you can spend a couple days to come down and look over our records and try to straighten them out." I said of course I would do that because I was connected with many of the gifts made by Republic Steel.

About that time, I mentioned to Charlie that he and Republic might want to have an honorary professorship at Case and I suggested that it could be Dr. Al Troiano, who was one of the world's foremost metallugists which was one of the important areas at Republic Steel and he said that he thought that was a good idea. It didn't take very long for Republic to make Al an honorary professor, which was good for Republic Steel, too, because they received publicity all over the world. For example, Dr. Troiano was the keynote speaker before the French Atomic Energy Commission in 1965.

Around the same time, the metallurgy building at Case was built and named the White Building in honor of Charlie White.

As mentioned before, we took several bids, usually three, on any major expenditure for Case which could be packaged. One of the major expenditures around this time when we were building a lot of buildings, was for steel shelving, and as usual we took three bids. U.S. Steel substantially underbid Republic Steel for the shelving. It was subsequently ordered from U. S. Steel and Charlie heard about it and called me and said, "Jim, I understand you have a substantial amount of U.S. Steel shelving that has been ordered for your new buildings." And I said, "Yes Charlie, we took our usual three bids and U.S. Steel was below Republic."

He said, "Jim, I don't want any U. S. Steel shelves out there at Case and I'll call down to our people and tell them to give you the shelving. But from now on, just give me a call and we'll see that Republic Steel gives you the best deal.

Another major influence on the Golden Years of Philanthropy was the philanthropy of the Smith family. It was my privilege to interact with the Smith family not only at Case Institute but at the Health Museum, Lake Erie College, the Museum of Natural History, and the Garden Center, now known as the Cleveland Botanical Gardens. I didn't have any direct involvement with their interest in the Sight Center but that was one of Eleanor Smith's principal interests. The family included Professor Smith, who I've already mentioned, who was the professor at Case; Kelvin and Kent Smith, who were his sons; Eleanor Smith, who was Kelvin's wife; Thelma Smith, who was Kent's wife; and Kelvin and Eleanor's daughters, Lucia and Cara. (Kelvin and Eleanor had a retarded son, Armstrong, who came to Cleveland periodically from a facility where he lived in the East.) Kent didn't have any children in Cleveland. A third brother, Vincent Smith, did not participate in all of the family wealth because he was a lawyer who chose to start his career with his in-laws' electrical company and so he didn't participate in the wealth that was created by the founding of Lubrizol Corporation. The original wealth of the family came because of Professor Smith's involvement with Herb Dow, the founder of Dow Chemical Co. The family always considered that Professor Smith, who taught Herb Dow, was one of the founders of Dow. Also, Kelvin, during some of the summers when he was a student at Case, spent time at Dow. One of the interesting things that Eleanor told me was that she had an opportunity to marry any of the Smith boys, but she always thought Kelvin was the "big catch." However, she also confided that the Smith boys were not in any way comparable to their father.

Kent was on the Case board, but Kelvin was not, because the president of Case felt that having two brothers on the board was not good policy. However, I took the position that Kelvin ought to be on the board because while both brothers were substantial donors to Case, Kelvin actually gave more. I kept suggesting that Kelvin ought to be on the board until one day Fred Crawford said to me, "You know, Jim, I think you're right. Kevin (Fred always called

Kelvin, Kevin) ought to be on the board." And in due course, he was elected to the board. I think it was one of my best contributions to Case.

Kelvin Smith thought Fred Crawford was one of the greatest, as I do, but Kent was less complimentary about Fred. Kent and Fred certainly knew each other and Fred knew of the great contributions of Kent to Case. He often told the story about how, before the first campaign for Case, he made a speech to the trustees and ended with the fact that he felt so supportive of Case and its importance to Cleveland that he would match the gift of any trustee. At that point, the way Fred put it, "This little fellow (Kent) stood up in the back of the room and said, 'I'll give $75,000'" (which was a great deal of money at that time). And Fred always concluded this story by saying, "I'll never do that again!"

Eleanor Smith had a great sense of humor and was a very interesting woman. One of her greatest interests was the Garden Center. The Garden Center had a long history of conducting a "white elephant" sale wherein it sold gifts of garden sculpture, clothes, and other interesting items received as gifts from the top society women and other Clevelanders, including Eleanor Smith. She volunteered and served in various capacities to make the white elephant sale a success. The Smiths also were major donors to the Garden Center.

When I became a consultant to the Garden Center and we conducted a major campaign, we made our campaign report meetings interesting by asking the various prominent Garden Center members to make presentations as part of the report meetings.

I suggested that we ask Eleanor Smith to make one of those presentations. We did, and she agreed. Later, when it came time for the report meeting and the speech, we had a head table set up and I and Elizabeth Chamberlain and the director of the Garden Center, Elliot Paine, sat at the head table along with Eleanor. I said, "Eleanor, we're going to have box lunches at this report meeting and you're probably not used to box lunches." She was very gracious and had a great sense of humor and she said," Jim, this is Thursday, and Thursday is the cook's day off and so I'm sure the box lunch will be much better fare than what I would have gotten at home." She then proceeded to give a terrific speech which ended with some stories about how the society women served in those early white elephant sales. She said one of the things that they counted on each year was the sale of various dresses that the women gave to the white elephant sale. A gentleman always came early and bought the whole batch of dresses and she said that they wondered over the years what he did with them. Then somebody said they thought they knew the answer. They said that the gentleman ran a bawdy house in Cleveland and he bought the dresses for the girls in the bawdy house! And Eleanor said that from then on, they had a special song which they sang as a group while they tended to their duties at the white elephant sale. And then she proceeded to sing the song as the last part of her speech. It was, "I Wonder Who's Wearing Them Now," to the tune of "I Wonder Who's Kissing Her Now."

She once said to me, "Jim, I bet you know all of the "stories" about the Smith family.

Lucia Smith Nash and Cara Smith Stirn became important leaders of the Kelvin and Eleanor Smith Foundation, and later, Ellen Stirn Mavec, daughter of Howard and Cara Stirn, has become prominently involved.

Kent and Thelma founded the 1525 Foundation and its outgrowth, The Second Foundation.

Kent was the older brother and was considered the organization man at Lubrizol. Kelvin, who was second in his class at Dartmouth (Professor Smith had his two sons go to Dartmouth after Case Institute because he felt they ought to have a liberal arts education as well as the engineering education) was a brilliant chemist. In my opinion, the relationship of Kelvin and Kent was a typical older brother/younger brother situation, and after their marriages, I think that they tended to drift apart because of the different relationships of the women they married.

Before they founded Lubrizol, Kent told me that he worked at various jobs and tried different things. In fact, he said that since his dad had told him that only one out of ten businesses succeeded, he decided to start twelve to make sure that one of them succeeded. Among other things, he was the developer of the Alcazar Hotel in the University Circle which is designed, I understand, much like one of the hotels which the Smith family stayed in during some of their travels.

When Keith Glennan, the president of Case, went to Washington for two years to be the head of NASA, Kent, who was just retiring as chairman of Lubrizol, took over as interim president. Being rather shy, he had many trepidations about being able to do the job. When he had to make his first presentation to the entire student body, he came over to my office and said that he didn't know what he should say. I said, "Kent, nobody can do it better than you, just tell them about your long relationship with Case." And that is what he did. He started out by saying that he used to, as a little boy, sit on the lap of the Case president at that time, and continued relating his relationship from that time on.

There is a history of Lubrizol written by several people but finally edited by my friend, John Baird, who was an executive at Lubrizol. John joined with Alex Nason, in the early days, to buy the Lubrizol retail operation, which was a very small portion of the company and was originally designed just to give them a little money to invest in the days when they needed money to keep the company going. John Baird became Alex Nason's best friend over the years. They divided the country in two and each took one-half to retail the products from Lubrizol. They soon became independently wealthy as a result, even though they also received much of their wealth from their positions at Lubrizol Corp.

When the history was completed, Kelvin Smith asked me what I thought of it, and I said, "I thought it was very interesting because I knew all the people involved." And I said, "What do you think, Kelvin?" He said, "There is too much of the Smiths in the history and not enough of Alex Nason. In the early days, Alex was everything." Later when I became more involved with Alex Nason as a result of several clients, Alex invited us to Lyford Key, which is a very beautiful resort in the Bahamas. Alex, who had a house on Nassau Island, came to meet us at the airport and I told him that story. And he said, "Jim, that's not right. Kelvin was the most important man -- he was the 'bench man'" (meaning that he conducted the laboratory research). When I later mentioned that to Kelvin, he said, "No that's not right. Most of the early bench work was done by Carl Prutton who was a professor at Case." Over the years, the Smith brothers made gifts to Case in honor of Alex and Alex made gifts to Case in honor of the Smiths. I'll leave it to others to figure out who was most important.

But certainly, Lubrizol was very important to Case. At one point Lubrizol hired Roger Clapp from Case and because they were taking one of Case's important professors, they said that they would never forget Case. Many times during the ensuing years when we wanted to make a proposal to Lubrizol for support and it didn't look like Lubrizol was going to provide the funds, Kent would say,"You know, those young Turks out there who are running the show now just don't realize how important Case is, and has been, to Lubrizol."

When Kent finished his interim presidency of Case, I suggested that we do something in his honor, and we made an arrangement to have one of the leading portrait artists in Cleveland, Mrs. Wright, paint Kent's portrait. Because the price was going to be about $5,000, I sent a little note to the various chairmen of the Case Associates' corporations. I said what I was going to do and asked them to send me a gift to pay for the honor to Kent which they promptly did. I quickly had the $5,000. However, I had a call from Kelvin Smith and he said, "Jim, send all the money back. No one can pay for a portrait in honor of my brother. I'll send you the money for the portrait," which he did, and I sent all of the money back.

To underscore the relationship of the brothers, one time Kelvin asked me, "What do you think Kent thinks of you?" And I said, "Well, I'll be honest with you, I think he thinks I'm 'too tough.'" Kelvin replied, "Don't let that worry you, he thinks I'm too tough too."

In the 60's I had a call from Thelma Smith, who said, "I'm worried about Kent, I don't think he's very well, so take it easy on him and don't give him too much to do." And I said I would certainly do that. But shortly after that, Frank Joseph called and said that he was going to recommend Kent for board membership at the Museum of Natural History. I told him that Thelma was worried about Kent's health. Frank forged ahead anyway and asked Kent, and Kent agreed. When I later mentioned that to Thelma, she said, "There wasn't anything I could do. He has this long interest in natural history." I became a consultant to the Museum of Natural History many times, and an old acquaintance, Art Dougan, who is on the Museum board, has written a history which covers those early relationships. It should be added to this overview.

I had found a document in the Case files that said that if Case would work out some arrangement with the Museum of Natural History in the area of astronomy, Mr. Boynton Murch, Sr., the father of Bud Murch and the grandfather of the now chairman of the board of the Museum of Natural History, would give $300,000. I couldn't see why that couldn't be worked out and proceeded to do so.

When Kent Smith got involved with the Museum of Natural History, he soon became one of their most important trustees. However, he didn't get along with Bill Scheele, who was the director of the Museum of Natural History at that time, and Kent asked if I would sit in at lunches with the two of them to act as a "referee." I did.

Later on when I had an office in the National City Bank Building, a rather interesting event transpired. Kent and Thelma's lawyers also had their offices in the National City Bank Building. Kent came down to my office with Phil Ranney, who was an assistant to Hubert Schneider, a partner in the firm of Schneider, Quail, and Henderson, who were very close to Kent. Phil looked frightened, and Kent said, "Jim, I want you to witness this, I'm taking the Museum of Natural History out of my will." And he looked at me to see what my reaction was and said, "I see that you don't like that." And I said, "No, I don't think that's a very nice thing to do, Kent." And he said, "Don't worry about it, I'll put them back in." Since then, many millions of dollars have been given by that side of the Smith family to the Museum of Natural History.

I had a fine relationship with Kent's lawyer, Hubert Schneider, which had some interesting ramifications. Almost in the first week when I came to Cleveland, I had a call from Hubert and he said he would like to take me to lunch, which he did. And when we went to lunch, he told me a very interesting story. He said that while he was a managing partner of a fine law firm and felt that the briefs that he wrote were very good, that his first love, rather than the law, was that he would have liked to be a writer. He said that he had a lifelong interest in Pepys and *Pepys' Diary* and he had traveled to all the places that Pepys talks about in his diary. He said that he had heard that I studied with Percy Hunt, the great professor at the University of Pittsburgh, and while he knew Hunt was an expert on Shakespeare and on "description and narration," he was also the world's leading expert on Pepys, and he'd like to meet him. So I arranged for Hubert to meet with Dr. Hunt, and it certainly was a good start with somebody who was so important to the Smiths and to Lubrizol. Later, Hubert told me that he could tell the proposals which I had something to do with because they were the only ones he could "understand."

I worked with Vincent Smith when I was a consultant to Hillcrest Hospital. Vincent was one of their most important patients. The way I became a consultant to Hillcrest Hospital was very unusual. I had a call from the Hillcrest executive who said that they were building a major wing and that in the proposal they had presented to the state to get approval to build the wing, the trustees had said that they would raise a million dollars. He said the wing was almost built and they hadn't yet done anything about the million dollars. They had completed the wing and saved enough money to pay for it, and there were several trustees who just wanted to forget about the million dollars. But at least two of the trustees were Case graduates, and "dug in" and said if the trustees didn't do what they said they would do, they would resign from the board. They also suggested that they should call Jim Hardie and raise the million dollars. And that's how I got connected with Hillcrest Hospital. They called me and I became a consultant. Vincent gave $100,000 that got us started on the campaign which was ultimately successful.

Cara and Howard Stirn (Kelvin's and Eleanor's daughter and son-in-law) were interested in Hawken and were very helpful when I became a consultant to Hawken School. They were also interested in the Museum of Natural History and Cara was on the steering committee of many of the campaigns I directed at the Museum over the years.

When Kelvin Smith retired from the chairmanship of Lubrizol he was replaced by Tom Mastin. Kelvin and I began to meet regularly about every two weeks for lunch. He said the only stipulation he wanted me to be aware of was that he had gotten up for breakfast meetings long enough and was only going to meet for lunch.

One time I stopped at his house on Shaker Boulevard and met with him in his study. He had a telephone call and asked me to stay. The telephone call went on for perhaps ten minutes. And when he concluded he said to me, "That was somebody who wants some money, but I've already made a gift and they didn't seem to know that." And I said, "Kelvin, are you always that kind with somebody who's obviously not prepared when they're asking for money?" And he said, "I try to be."

The Smiths became interested in aquariums and were, I think, owners of "Mystic" in Connecticut. I think this was a result of the fact that Howard had a Ph.D. in oceanography and had a small plant in Florida which manufactured seawater for use in aquariums. At one of our luncheons, Kelvin asked me if I would consider running their various interests in aquariums and I told him immediately that I appreciated the fact that he thought so well of me to offer the job, but I was very content with what I was doing. I think he expected that would be my answer.

Kent Smith picked up the "matching gift" philosophy that I had helped develop in Cleveland and used it in many of the things he was interested in. Early on, even though I had been a consultant to the Museum of Natural History, and actually helped them set up their first annual fund, the Museum of Natural History wanted to do a major $8 million campaign and they didn't ask me to be a consultant. I think they planned to do it themselves which was always my advice, that the best way to do it was to do it themselves if they could. They went to Kent and asked him for a major gift toward that $8 million campaign. Kent turned them down. They quickly called me and said they wanted to meet with me. They outlined how they asked him, and I said, 'You didn't ask him right. I know how Kent looks at these sorts of things." I pulled out an envelope and said, "If you really want to get a major gift from Kent, this is how I think you ought to do it." I said, "Number one, you ought to figure out how much your trustees other than Kent can give and ask him to make a gift, perhaps a million dollars, if the trustees will give a million, and secondly, do the same thing for the corporations and foundations, and then thirdly, ask him to match all the other gifts, too." I said, "Thus, you might ask him for as much as $3 million." They were elated and after a short time they called me and said that Kent had agreed to match the trustees up to a million and the corporations and foundations up to another million and all other gifts up to a third million. Finally, if they were successful, he would give another million -- in other words, $4 million out of the $8 million. They asked me to be a consultant again. I agreed and we conducted a campaign for $8 million which was a success. The leaders were Bud Murch, Newman Halvorson, and David Ingalls.

Up to that time, Kent was quite vehement that he didn't want any memorials in honor of him, and Kelvin was of the same feeling.

Kent took me aside one day and said, "I think I've been wrong, I've given away all this money and nobody knows who I am." So I said to the Museum of Natural History, "Why don't we do a memorial to Kent, or a tribute, and I have a feeling that he might change his mind." The Museum decided to create the Wildflower Garden in honor of Kent and Thelma who were very pleased.

During this time several other relationships developed with Kelvin Smith. The first one occurred when Kelvin asked me to meet with him, Paul Frohring, who was one of the wealthiest men in Cleveland, and Darwin Noll, chairman of Cardinal Corporation, at the Hunt Club, which is a prominent club in the area east of Cleveland. When we met, they said they were having a campaign at the Health Museum where they were on the board and they had hired a person who I would describe as talented but who was really not a professional, as a consultant to the campaign. The campaign had fallen far short of the goal and they wanted me to fix it up. Starting over after failing is one of the most difficult jobs to do. I had known Paul Frohring for some time and while I didn't know Darwin Noll at that time, he said that he would be glad to be campaign chairman and do anything I wanted him to. What it really amounted to was that they were "ordering" me to be a consultant, and I had no choice.

Paul Frohring, on the day that I announced that I was leaving Case and going into the consulting business, read the story in the paper and made several calls to me but I was busy and couldn't return them. When I returned the calls about eight o-clock that evening, I apologized and he said, "Oh Jim, it wasn't that urgent, I just wanted to be the first one to give you a client." I never forgot that.

Many years later, Paul told me he'd like to get his wife, Maxine, involved with one of my campaigns and she joined the steering committee of the Garden Center Campaign and Paul gave $100,000.

Later, Kelvin asked me to lunch and said that he had a very important problem that he wanted me to address concerning Lake Erie College. I was not a consultant to Lake Erie College at that time but I had been a consultant for one day as a result of a call from Elden Winkler who was vice president for development at Lake Erie College. He said that he wanted me to meet with him, the president of Lake Erie College, Paul Weaver, and Jim Lincoln, who was chairman of Lincoln Electric Company and also chairman of the board of the College. When I got to the meeting, Jim Lincoln said that he wanted me to answer just one question and for that he would pay my full consulting fee. And I said, "Well, you don't have to do that, but what's the question?" He said, "We want to have a campaign for Lake Erie College and I want to know who would be best to be chairman of the campaign." And I said, "Jim, that's a very simple question and I can give you a quick answer. You should be chairman." He said, "Fine." And that was the end of the meeting and he became chairman of the campaign. Later on I became a consultant to Lake Erie College many times over the years.

There are many stories that can be told about Jim Lincoln. One of the stories which indicates something about the character of Jim Lincoln occurred when his brother John had started a little company called Lincoln Electric in Cleveland and Jim was in college at Ohio State. He was a tall, well-built young man and was the star fullback at Ohio State. He also was very bright and in one of his classes asked a question which the professor judged to be impertinent. It wasn't impertinent, and when Jim took offense, the professor started proceedings to have Jim thrown out of school.

When the coaches heard that their star fullback had been expelled, they started an effort to have him reinstated. Finally, they agreed on what they wanted to do and they sent the Dean to talk to Jim and tell him that all he had to do was apologize to the professor and they would allow him back in school. When they told Jim, he answered, "Me apologize to him? He should apologize to me." So Jim packed his bag and went up to Cleveland where he joined his brother at Lincoln Electric. Several years later, the company was doing very well and Jim was one of the top donors at Ohio State. "Boss Kettering" was also one of the large donors to Ohio State, and Ohio State decided to give both Jim and Kettering honorary degrees.

Subsequently, they called Jim and told him they wanted to give him an honorary degree and he said, "Give me an honorary degree? I never got my first degree." That problem was settled by giving Jim Lincoln both his undergraduate degree and an honorary degree at the same time.

I hosted Jim Lincoln at various affairs at Case which I enjoyed immensely and I got to know him very well.

Lincoln Electric was a major donor to Case and when major gifts came in, we had a system for acknowledging them. I would dictate the acknowledgment for the president's signature which he would sign and send. In all major gifts, I endeavored to dictate especially appropriate letters. In one of these letters to Jim, after some appropriate introductory paragraphs, I ended the letter with a sentence, "We will work harder than ever to merit your continued support." After a week or so, the president called me and said, "I saw Jim Lincoln today and he said that my acknowledgment letter for Lincoln Electric's recent gift was really a masterpiece." And then he said, "Jim, what did I say?"

I knew that the prompt and pertinent acknowledgment process was a very important part of the development system.

Kelvin Smith called me several years later to talk about Lake Erie College. He said that he had become interested in the college because they had a good equestrian program. Kelvin and his family had long been interested in horses and riding, and both the daughters and Kelvin were excellent horsemen. The reason he wanted to talk to me was that he had made a sizeable gift to Paul Weaver, the president of Lake Erie College, to build an equestrian center on the Morley Farm which is a beautiful farm including the Morley Mansion, that had been given to Lake Erie College.

Kelvin said that the equestrian center was partially completed and that he, Kelvin, would have no more to do with it. In a sense, he was washing his hands of it. He said that if I became a consultant and I needed somebody from the Smith family to help, he suggested his eldest daughter, Lucia, who he thought would benefit by being associated with one of my campaigns.

When I went to the college to get brought up to date, Paul Weaver took me to Morley Farm and showed me what they had done. There was a huge skeleton of a building with just the steel beams showing but nothing much more. I said, "Paul, I think there's some problem, would you mind telling me what it is?" And he said, "Jim, I never got approval from the board of trustees to construct this building and Bill Irrgang (whom I knew because of my work at Case, then chairman of Lincoln Electric and chairman of the board of Lake Erie College) is dead set against horses. In fact he says that anybody who gets on the back of a horse is a damn fool. So I don't know what to do." I said, "What I foresee, Paul, is a big story in the Painesville paper in the not too distant future: "Lonely 'Turkey' standing on Morley Farm." He asked me to be a consultant and get him out of the "mess."

I certainly didn't like the fact that the trustees hadn't approved the equestrian center and I told Kelvin Smith that I would help out but I wouldn't take any money for the consulting. I then met with Frank Milbourne, chairman of Coe Manufacturing Co., who was on the Lake Erie College board and one of the finest men I've ever met.

I knew him very well because of my friendship with Art Holden who was vice president of Coe Manufacturing Co. and a prominent Case alumnus. I told Frank that in my opinion, the college was in trouble and if we were to come out of this dilemma we had to get approval of the board of trustees to conduct a campaign for the Equestrian Center. Frank said that there wasn't one chance in fifty that approval could be gotten because of Bill Irrgang's attitude. I said, "Riding on the back of a horse isn't any crazier than hitting and chasing a little white golf ball." I said that I thought that he was the only person that could talk to Bill Irrgang and resolve the issue. He did, reluctantly, and he came back to me and said that Irrgang had approved of the equestrian campaign but "the trustees would take no part in it" (which went against all the principles of fundraising). I decided that the best thing I could do was give it a try.

We put together a campaign steering committee which included Lucia Nash (Kelvin Smith's daughter), George Humphrey's daughter-in-law, Lulu, who had been a champion horsewoman, and Oliver Bolten, the son of Francis Paine Bolten, who was a member of the House of Representatives and one of the leaders of the Cleveland community.

Several things are interesting about Oliver (we called him "Ollie") Bolten. We became good friends and later he said to me, "Jim, I'll back you and we can form a national fundraising company and you can be the head of it." I said, "Ollie, I've done that before. I owned part of one of the big fundraising firms and the administration sits in the back room and shuffles people all over the country. I have more fun and feel I can do more good out on the firing line."

Ollie had a great respect for George Humphrey, and so did Kelvin Smith. Kelvin thought that George Humphrey was one of the finest persons he had ever known and made much of the fact that George was the only person in Cleveland to be elected twice to the honor of Nicey Prias. Nicey Prias was an affair held every year by the lawyers of Cleveland and included the election of the top citizen of the year. It also included a roast, which was funny, written by the lawyers.

James C. Hardie

We soon began to make real headway on the Equestrian Center campaign and I said it was very important that all the members of the committee make their gifts. Ollie Bolten said, "Jim, I know I live like a feudal baron but I really don't have that much money." I assumed that what he was saying was that his assets were mostly in the trusts which had been set up by his mother. I said, "Ollie, if you don't make a gift, it will influence everybody else on this committee and we will fail. Knowing that I'm doing this campaign without any fee and how important it is to Lake Erie College, I propose that if you don't make a gift, you suggest a memorial to me on the Lake Erie campus, and it can be a 'horse's ass'." He called me the next day and said that he had changed his mind and had decided to make a gift. (To my recollection it was $25,000.)

The campaign succeeded and the equestrian center was named the George M. Humphrey Equestrian Center. We had a grand dedication affair and my recollection is that Ollie Bolten agreed to be master of ceremonies, although he said originally that he didn't think he would be able to get emotionally through a dedication in honor of George M. Humphrey.

In my opinion, the Equestrian Center saved Lake Erie College because the college was able to put on a vast promotion for women students who had horses which they could bring to Lake Erie College. Later I was called on several times to help save Lake Erie College which always seemed to be in financial difficulty and in need of students to survive.

In my opinion the Equestrian Center contributed to the problems of Lake Erie College as well as helping solve them. As a result of the campaign for the Equestrian Center, Lincoln Electric and Bill Irrgang and Bill Irrgang's successor, Ted Willis, who had been bailing out Lake Erie College for years (because of the early association with Jim Lincoln who married the dean of Lake Erie College), decided that the prominent families that had supported the Equestrian Center should also take a greater part in supporting Lake Erie College.

At that time, Cyrus Eaton was on the Case board and he got into a substantial disagreement with George Humphrey over the St. Lawrence Seaway. It was evident that Cy's opposition to George Humphrey had resulted in the leadership of Cleveland being opposed to Eaton and supportive of George Humphrey. It became evident that Cy Eaton's membership on the Case board was going to cause a great number of problems for Case. I didn't know Cy Eaton that well but in all my dealings with him (most of them were over the phone) he conscientiously did whatever I asked him to do and then would report to me that it had been done.

Later I had a call from a woman who was the head of the Hudson Library board asking for my advice and said that they had a program to renovate the library that would cost $75,000. She said the consultant firm that they had hired said that they should campaign not for the $75,000 that they needed but since they were charging $50,000 for their services, they proposed a campaign for $125,000. I thought that was "obscene" and said that I couldn't get involved and didn't want to get involved, but I would propose a way they could raise the money and save the $50,000 they were going to pay to the consulting firm. She asked me what I would propose, and I said, "First of all go to John Ong, the chairman of Goodrich Corp., and ask him to ask for $10,000 each from three foundations," and I named them. I knew that John Ong was on the board of the three foundations and I said I thought John Ong would agree to do that because he lived in Hudson and I had been to his house and he had more books than I have. She said, "Isn't that interesting, Mr. Ong used to be president of the library." She then said, "What do we do if we get the $30,000?" I said, "Go to your board of trustees and ask them to match the $30,000; if they do, you'll have $60,000, and then you can campaign for the last $15,000."

Some time passed and she called me and said, "We want you to come down to Hudson so we can honor you." I said, "For what?" And she said because it worked just like you said it would. "We now have the $75,000." I said, "You don't have to have any celebrations for me, I think it's great that you did it, but you might want to honor John Ong." She then said, "I didn't tell you when I called, but I know you." And I said, "I'm embarrassed because I certainly don't remember you." She said, "There's no way you would, but I was secretary to Cy Eaton during those years when you were at Case and I always made his calls and I always thought that you were nice and so that's how I know you."

Ralph Besse told me about Cy Eaton's testimony in connection with Cy Eaton's Canadian Penny stock trial. Ralph Besse is a lawyer who became chairman of CEI after Elmer Lindseth. Ralph said that when they were questioning Cy Eaton, he took sort of a prayerful position with his hands clasped together. He was an imposing looking man and quite a scholar. (He had started out as secretary to John D. Rockefeller, I think, in Cleveland, and then went on to be one of Cleveland's and the nation's prominent financiers.) At the Canadian trial they asked Cy Eaton how you go about taking over a company (which he was very good at). And he very quietly said, "Well," taking that prayerful look, "the first thing you have to do is buy the management."

Incidentally, Ralph Besse is a very interesting story in himself. He was born on a farm in southern Ohio and got a scholarship to Heidelberg College in Tiffin, Ohio. He told me that when he went to Heidelberg for the first time for his freshman year, he didn't have any extra clothes beyond the ones he was wearing and he was a little embarrassed about that so he went up to Heidelberg carrying an empty suitcase.

Ralph told me that story when we flew together to New York City, and as we traded stories, he was one of the first people to urge me to write a book and include the stories about important people I had known. Ralph went on to the University of Michigan after Heidelberg to get a law degree. I asked Elmer Lindseth how he chose Ralph to follow him as chairman of CEI. Elmer said it was not difficult at all. He noticed that every time he set up an important committee at CEI, he would ask the chairman who he wanted to be on his committee, and almost everyone chose as their first choice, Ralph Besse.

Later, I was privileged to be a consultant to Ursuline College when they conducted a campaign to build a library in honor of Ralph Besse.

But getting back to the George Humphrey - Cy Eaton problem, I called Fred Crawford and he came out to my office. I said, "The consensus seems to be that we should ask Cy Eaton to leave the board of Case and I don't know anybody else who could do that job except you, Fred." He thought about it for a moment and he said, "I'll do it." A few days lapsed and he came back and said, "I went to see Cy Eaton and I told him that he was causing problems for Case and Cy said, 'Oh Frederic, I certainly don't want to do any harm to Case' and he agreed to resign from the board."

Bill Irrgang, for whom I had a great deal of respect, was a very tough executive. An indication of how tough he was, when Paul Weaver asked me to become a consultant to Lake Erie College after the Equestrian Center Campaign, I proposed that Lake Erie start an annual fund and I got them a development director to help carry out the suggestions that I would make relative to the annual fund. One of the first things I suggested was that we needed a top-flight chairman of the annual fund and I met with Bill Irrrgang to talk about the proposed plans. Bill asked me who I thought would make a first-rate chairman, and I said Ted Willis, who at that time was executive vice president of Lincoln Electric. And Bill said, "You got him." And I said, "What do you mean, Bill, we haven't asked him yet?" And he said, "Just ask him; I know he'll say yes." And I said, "How can you be so sure?" And he said, "I'll tell him that if he wants to be president of this company, he better say yes."

Frank Milbourne told me that many times Lake Erie College would go into its commencement ceremony with a deficit of perhaps $600,000 and they would not know whether Lincoln Electric and Bill Irrgang were going to do anything about it until the actual commencement program was being conducted and all of the trustees were sitting up on the stage. Bill Irrgang would then pass a note to Frank which said, "We'll pick up the deficit." Milbourne would pass a note to President Paul Weaver which would not only save Lake Erie College but would also save Paul Weaver!

I had a long relationship with Paul Weaver and it was always interesting. He had a tremendous fear of Bill Irrgang because of what Irrgang could do to him and Paul could never understand how

I could walk into Bill Irrgang's office and talk to him with such ease. And I guess the answer was that I liked Bill Irrgang, and I think he liked me.

Also, although I certainly couldn't condone many of the things that Paul Weaver did, I still had an amusing respect for him. One time he called me, greatly agitated, and said, "Can you meet me at the bar at the Hunt Club because I'm in deep trouble?" I did and when I got there he said, "Jim, there are things I have to do at Lake Erie College that are not the most acceptable and one of them is that we've been running the electricity for the Morley Mansion (where Paul and his wife lived) from the Equestrian Center. Ernst & Ernst, who are our auditors, are taking the stance that they're not going to approve this year's annual report because I should have paid for the electricity. If they don't approve this report, I'll be out of here and who knows what will happen to Lake Erie College." I thought awhile and said, "Paul, who does Lincoln Electric's audit and annual report?" And he said, "Ernst & Ernst." And I said, "Therein I think lies the solution." Paul, being a very bright guy, got the point. Looking back, I'm not exactly proud of that solution, because Ernst & Ernst were my friends.

I'll cover many more efforts in connection with Lake Erie College later in this book which I hope will be interesting because they are still interesting to me, years later.

Kelvin Smith never forgot that I "bailed out" the Equestrian Center and the Lake Erie College problem. Later, he sent me a year-end gift of $3,000 which was the amount that could be given as a tax deductible gift to family members at that time.

The *Cleveland Magazine* called me and said that they were doing a story on the Smith brothers (Kelvin, Kent, and Vincent) and that they wanted to make sure that they had the facts straight and wondered if I would check the story.

I surmised that the brothers had been contacted and refused to be interviewed. I knew how they felt about privacy so I said I didn't think I could do that because I didn't think the Smiths wanted the publicity. The editor of the magazine got quite irate and said, "You mean someone like you who is in public relations won't help another organization who is also allied with public relations?" And I said, "I know how you feel but I'm certain that the Smiths want to keep their privacy."

Subsequently, I saw Kelvin and told him that the *Cleveland Magazine* had called and what I had said and what I had done.

He said, "Don't worry about it, Jim, but now I'll have to hire some more people to protect my family." The story did run in due course and I think I have a copy somewhere in my files.

In the early days of the 50 Golden Years when we were just beginning to research foundations and make foundation proposals, I heard that the attorney general kept a list of all the Ohio 1090's (I think that was the way the reports from foundations were designated in the attorney general's office). And I found out that the attorney general would send copies of them to anyone who wanted them for about 25¢ or 50¢ apiece. So I called the attorney general's office and got a large box with hundreds of foundation reports which were very valuable to me in searching out where we might make special proposals for my clients.

The reports listed the foundation trustees, how much money they had, and where they made their gifts and where their interests were.

One day, Kent Smith stopped by the office and said that the reports were a very valuable resource. Not too much later, he asked me if he could borrow my box of foundation records and that box became the database of what is now known as the Kent Smith Foundation Center.

During this time, Fred Crawford remained chairman of the Case board and we scheduled meetings when he was in town, but we continued to function successfully under the philanthropic "aura" which he had created.

Also during this entire time, Hassel Tippit, the managing partner of Ernst & Ernst, was chairman of the development committee. He was called "the world's best accountant" yet he repeatedly told me that he couldn't speak for Case "academically" because he was not a college graduate. He would only say that, "Case is a well-run business." My rejoinder was, "Tip, you're so smart that you didn't have to go to college."

He didn't complete high school until after he came to Cleveland from Nashville, Tennessee as a young man. (He did get a high school diploma later, I think, by correspondence.) He told me that he had two good opportunities when he was in high school in Nashville, Tennessee: He could come to Cleveland as an apprentice to Mr. Ernst, the managing partner of Ernst & Ernst, or he could play semi-pro baseball. I asked him about the baseball and he answered with the only boast I ever heard him utter. He said, "Jim, I could hit anybody!" I was told that he gave brilliant testimony in the Canadian Penny stock trial on behalf of Cyrus Eaton. In the 60's the newspapers reported that Tip was the highest paid man in Ohio at around $580,000 a year which, at that time, was a tremendous amount of money. One time when he was sitting beside me at one of the campaign report meetings at Case, he quietly wrote out a check for $40,000 and handed it to me.

He was a good friend of Claude Foster, a well-known philanthropist who donated many church organs throughout Ohio. When Claude Foster was dying, Tip would go out and sit at his bedside.

At one of our Case development committee meetings, we were sitting around a low cocktail table and I was using one corner of the table for my papers and Tip was on the opposite corner, about five or six feet away. After the meeting he whispered to me, "I think, Jim, one of your figures was wrong." And I said, "Tip, can you read upside down across a table?" And he said, "Jim, if you had sat across the desk from as many corporate board chairmen as I have, you'd learn to read upside down, too."

The attendance at Case development committee meetings was great and I'm certain that it was largely due to Fred Crawford's influence and also, Tip's. I remember, when we added Willard Brown to the committee, his reaction to his first meeting. He was vice president of Clevite and husband of Louise Ingalls, putting together two fine Cleveland families, the Ingalls and the Browns. When Willard attended his first development committee meeting, we followed our usual routine. I usually would have a list of foundations, corporations, or individuals to whom I wanted to make proposals for major grants. What I was looking for in each instance was a personal association between a committee member and the person who controlled each of the prospects. When I would mention a top prospect, usually one on the committee would say, "I can take that." Then in the near future that trustee would personally make an appointment with the prospect and present our proposal. This personal approach was the key to our unique success and proved again that, "People give to people."

When the meeting was over, Willard Brown pulled me aside and with considerable dismay, asked, "Jim, do those fellows always step up like that?" And I said, "Yes, they do." And I'm sure Willard realized that he was in for quite a job if he was going to try to equal the other members of our development committee.

Once, Tip asked me if I would drive to Tiffin, Ohio with him because he had been invited by the trustees of the Betty Jane Institution to visit that fine facility which is dedicated to helping handicapped children. While we were driving, I asked him about the Betty Jane Institution and he said he didn't know much about it but that Claude Foster had mentioned his interest in the institution. When we got there we were greeted effusively and taken on a tour. While we were walking around, the executive said to me, "Who is this guy?" I said, "He's Hassel Tippit, the Managing Partner of Ernst & Ernst." And he said, "We don't know anything about him except that he's our largest contributor!" Later I asked Tip about that and he said he had made a gift in honor of Claude Foster because his friend, Claude, had mentioned it.

While we were in Tiffin, I planned to talk to Robert Friedman, the head of National Machinery Company, who was a Case graduate and I was surprised that the Betty Jane Institution had substantial ties with National Machinery. National Machinery had founded Betty Jane Institution in honor of their founder's handicapped daughter. However, to indicate some of the problems you can have when you're trying to run a national educational institution, the Case man who ran National Machinery, Robert Friedman, had criticized Case by saying that we weren't producing graduates who could do the practical type of engineering jobs that students were taught to do when he was at Case. One of the statements that got back to us was that in his time, Case produced engineers who could feel (I assume he was talking about bearings) a thousandth of an inch on the ends of their fingertips.

In due course, I decided to check that out with Lou Tuve who was head of the Mechanical Engineering Department and recognized as a leading engineering professor.

I talked to him one day and asked him about feeling a thousandth of an inch on your fingertips. Lou, who had been a professor a long time, smiled and said, "You know, that's the kind of thing that you hear but really I don't know anybody who could feel a thousandth of an inch on the end of his fingertips nor could we have figured out a way to teach that."

Timken Corporation in Stark County, south of Cleveland, hired a sizeable number of Case graduates over the years and, using the list of graduates, we asked the Timken brothers, Henry and Bob, to come on the board at Case. They thought it over and said they couldn't do it but Herb Markley was going to be the next president of Timken, and they would urge him to come on the Case board if we asked him. We did, and Herb came on the board. One day he said to me, "Why is it that anytime academic economists are quoted in the papers, they always speak from the liberal side. Aren't there any prominent academic economists who are conservative?" I said, "Herb, why don't you do something about that. Give us an endowment for a professorship and we'll hire a prominent conservative economist." And he said, "I think we might do that."

Later on he said, "Why don't you make a proposal to Timken to fund a conservative professorship?" I told him at that time the amount of endowment which would produce enough income to pay the professor's salary and secretarial and other necessary support was $750,000 and he said that that would be okay.

I talked to Tip about the possible professorship and asked him if he knew the Timkins and he said, "Yes, I know the Timkens and I could go down with you and your people to make a presentation to

Bob and Henry Timken, but remember, I can't speak academically but I will say that Case is a well-run business." On the day we were going down to make the presentation, I heard that we would be competing with Harvard and that Harvard was going to have their president, the head of their medical school, and Neil MacElroy, the chairman of Proctor & Gamble in Cincinnati, helping present their proposal. Also, Fred Crawford was going to be there on Harvard's behalf because Fred had been an overseer at Harvard and was one of their oldest graduates!

We made our proposal, and Harvard made theirs. Henry and Bob then said they were going to meet immediately and make a decision and tell us about it. When it came time for Tip to speak, all Tip had said was, "Henry and Bob, I can tell you that Case is a well-run business."

We went outside and waited and in due course Henry and Bob came out and said, "Well, you fellows get the $750,000. We're giving Harvard $25,000." When I had a chance, I took Bob aside and said, "Bob, why did we get it?" And he said, "Oh, Jim, it was Tip. Tip has been a consultant with Timken for a great number of years, has given us three treasurers in that time, and never asked for anything. We just couldn't turn him down." And I said, "But he didn't ask for anything." And he said, "Yes, but he was sitting there."

Later, when I was a consultant to Hathaway Brown, I found that Mrs. Bob Timken had attended Hathaway Brown, the private school in Cleveland, and when we discovered this we were elated and made a presentation to the Timken Foundation, which had about $80 million at that time, one of the largest foundations in Ohio. We were surprised when we got a quick turn down. The refusal was from Mrs. Timken. I worked behind the scenes to have someone talk to Bob Timken and clandestinely we received a token gift from Bob for $25,000. I later found out that Mrs. Timken was sent up to Cleveland to Hathaway Brown to live and go to school. It's understandable that a young girl would not be happy (especially at that time) at being torn away from her family and sent to a boarding school. Apparently Mrs. Timken had no fond memories of her situation away from home.

One time when we were deliberating the investments of Case's endowment, which at that time was about $40 million, the banker advisors were suggesting a fairly substantial shift in our investment policies from conservative to liberal. The advisors wanted a substantial shift to more risky stocks. When it came time for Tip to give his opinion, he suggested the opposite direction and said that stocks were then valued at 15 or 20 times earnings and he didn't think that anything above ten times earnings was prudent. Fortunately for Case, Tip won the day and the endowment was invested in more conservative bonds. Shortly afterwards, there was a substantial downturn in the market and Tip turned out to be right

Tip had a son, Carlisle, who was a very successful entrepreneur. He founded a company called Mogul and became a substantial philanthropist. At the various social and fundraising affairs around Cleveland I would see him periodically and would always mention something about my relationship with his father.

But he never seemed to respond in a cordial fashion about these stories. However, he was always cordial to me.

Finally, one day after I had mentioned again a relationship or something I had done recently with Tip, Carlisle muttered, "I guess the old bastard does some good things."

I then knew that this was another example to Kelvin Smith's comment about the "testy" relationship of self-made men and their sons.

When Tip retired, Dick Baker succeeded as Managing Partner. Dick Baker had a great sense of humor and immediately became a leader in Cleveland. He had also been, I think, a star basketball player at Ohio State. I continued to meet with Tip from time to time but it was obvious that he had in mind going back to Nashville.

At one of our luncheons at the Union Club, I asked him how his retirement was going and I got less than a positive response. I said, "I know, Tip, that you know in all these turnovers of chairmanships there always seem to be problems." And he smiled and said, "Yes, but an amateur could do better!" When he left Cleveland, Cleveland lost a tremendous asset.

Relative to retiring leaders, Bob Fairbank, the chairman of Towmotor, told me at lunch one day that he was getting close to retiring as Towmotor chairman, and I said, "Bob, you better be prepared because I've noticed when top people retire they quickly lose their power and some of them don't realize that." Several months later he called me, after it had been in the Friday paper that he had retired. He called on Monday and said, "Jim, I know you told me that I would lose my power when I retired, but you didn't tell me that I wouldn't be able to get anybody to go to lunch with me."

It was evident that Case was heading toward another major campaign which would be national in scope and, although Fred Crawford still retained important influence in spite of his advanced age (he lived to 103), it was decided to make a Case graduate, Elmer Lindseth, chairman of the board.

During the Golden Years, Elmer Lindseth, the chairman of CEI, was very effective in the philanthropic area. He was not personally wealthy and the Cleveland Electric Illuminating Company didn't traditionally make "leadership" gifts, but Elmer changed that substantially.

He didn't have an automobile and lived close to the Rapid in Shaker Heights, so he took the Rapid down to the "Square" and walked over to his office. Often he would call me when he was going to Case for a trustees meeting and ask if he could hitch a ride home.

Our talks on those days were very interesting. For example, one day he asked me with astonishment, "Is it true that the Smiths (Kelvin and Eleanor) actually have a full-time gardener?" They did. One of those times he told me that he had found out that Fred Crawford's brother had worked for CEI for many years. I never mentioned this to Fred and he never mentioned it to me. The bottom line is -- I guess I felt that it was none of my business.

At a Case development committee meeting early in the Case $16 million campaign, Elmer Lindseth announced that CEI would pledge a half-million dollars. This was one of those "ten-strikes" coming at the right time which serve to move others who then make break-through leadership gifts that make a campaign successful.

Elmer received a scholarship to Case after attending either John Hay or Glenville High School, graduated from Case, and then went on and got a degree at Yale. He told me that his mother was a "domestic" and that out of his scholarship to Case he was able to save money to help out at home.

Indicative of Elmer's influence, I remember a meeting in connection with a Museum of Natural History campaign at the Union Club when we were discussing leadership gifts, and we wondered whether the Cleveland Foundation would be receptive to a major proposal early in the campaign. Elmer quickly left the Union Club room where we were meeting, made a call, and came back and said, "They will be supportive."

Along the way, Elmer had served as a president of the Case Associates. Once, when Em and I were at a party for one of the institutions in Cleveland, we sat at a table with one of Elmer's grandsons and I asked him whether he had seen his grandfather recently. He said that he had just come back from a vacation in Colorado with his grandfather and they had taken one of those raft "whitewater" trips down the Snake River. He said that while they were going down the river you could see the rock walls on each side and that his grandfather would call out the types of striated rock as they passed. And he, I think his name is Brian, said that he asked his grandfather, "How do you know so much about the rocks?" And Elmer answered him promptly, "Didn't you go to high school!"

During the early years of Elmer's chairmanship, Keith Glennan retired and Bob Morse was named president of Case.

At a trustees meeting, I suggested that we seek half a dozen professorships in honor of the new president. Elmer asked me somewhat incredulously, "Jim, who do you think is going to give these professorships." (At that time we were pricing professorships at $500,000.) I answered, "I think Bill Treuhaft would be a good candidate." Elmer said, "Jim, Bill doesn't have that kind of money." I answered, "As you know, I've worked closely with Bill, and I think he does."

Ultimately, Bill not only gave a professorship, but he gave two professorships. Using these two leadership gifts, we were able to solicit the half dozen professorships.

Elmer also became chairman of the $17 million campaign and carried on many of the discussions relative to the goal and with the Case Alumni Association. In the records which I have turned over to the Western Reserve Historical Society, there are many of the memos which resulted from those negotiations.

George Dively, chairman of Harris Corporation, provided key support to both Fred Crawford and Elmer Lindseth because many of his contributions to the golden years of philanthropy and his ability to cut to the heart of the matter and convince others, made him critically important at this time.

Many people didn't like George because he was so "tough." But I found that if he "knocked you down," which he did often, if you got up and gave him a good wallop, he respected you for it. He wrote a book on management, which was well received, and he devised what he called, "The Troika," system of management. He respected "judgment" more than intelligence. He told me that when he hired top employees for Harris Corporation, he hired them "forever." He said that he couldn't afford to lose any of them, and to my recollection, he succeeded. An example of this philosophy occurred when I was working with George on the Corporate 1% Program when he assigned Fred Baker, who worked in public relations for Harris Corporation, to assist me. One day when Fred and I were flying to New York to talk to the *New York Times* about the 1% Program, Fred said to me that he had decided to leave Harris Corporation and go to work for a company in Chicago which was allied to the philanthropic field. I said it was none of my business, but I didn't think it sounded like a very good idea. I told Fred that I thought he had made a mistake and when George Dively later asked me about it, I said that I thought Fred had made a mistake. A month or so passed and Fred called me and said, "Jim, you were right, I made a mistake." At that time I was with George Dively and he said, "What do you hear from your friend, Fred?" And I said, "I think he made a mistake and I think he knows it." And George said, "Do you think you could get him to have a beer with me?" And I said, "I think I can." I called Fred and he called George and later reported to me that George not only gave him the raise but made him director of corporate relations, which was one of the issues on the table when he left. Fred said that he was very grateful for what I had done but he said that George said, "Fred, once is enough!"

I remember there were certain days when George and I spent a lot of time together while traveling or dealing with important issues, and I was certain that during the entire day he didn't agree with anything that I said. (I mean that literally.) But we ended up respecting each other.

George graduated from the University of Pittsburgh with an engineering degree and also went to the Harvard Business School which led to the development of the Dively Entrepreneurship Award, which is a partnership between the Dively Foundation and the Harvard Business School Club of Northeastern Ohio. The first award was made in 1983 and the award dinner was attended by several hundred Harvard Business School graduates. The awards, which have continued, are granted to a company or individual in northeast Ohio who has demonstrated unusual success. Success is measured by rapid growth in size and profitability of the company over a recent five-year period as well as the achievement of a significant position in the marketplace.

The Dively Foundation, when I was a board member, gave $4 million to Case Western Reserve to build the George S. Dively Center which is a beautiful building that is part of the Weatherhead School, combining state-of-the-art classrooms and space which can be used to educate the hundreds of men and women who return to Case Western Reserve for updating in their chosen or other fields. I was especially gratified to be part of this gift because when I was vice president of Case Institute my office handled all of Case's special non-degree programs, even though the faculty members did all the teaching.

This was a time of great change in the entire national development area. The number of college students was projected to jump from six to twelve million, necessitating a vast increase in funding. George Dively said to me, "Jim, if you come up with an earth-shaking national idea or innovation in fundraising or development, I'll back you to the hilt." I agreed to do so.

I had read a speech by Frank Abrams, the chairman of Standard Oil of New Jersey, about corporate giving and the percentage of gifts by corporations. At that time corporations were giving about three-tenths of one percent of their domestic profits to higher education. After doing some figuring, I told George that I thought it might be possible to conduct a program calling for corporations to give one percent of their pre-tax profits to higher education. This was the amount they gave to *all* areas, including higher education. He thought it was a great idea and we set about working out a program to sell the idea. There was no doubt that this was an important national need. We came up with a two-page statement that outlined our objectives and why they were important. (The statement reads something like the Bill of Rights.)

We decided to try to promote a group of Cleveland corporations to take leadership in the "Corporate 1% Program." The plan called for corporations to make gifts to institutions anywhere in the country as long as they were to higher education. The gifts didn't have to include Case. I figured Case would get its share if the program succeeded.

Harris Corporation was the first corporation to agree to sign and my recollection is that TRW and Lubrizol followed closely. We knew we also needed a billion dollar corporation to prove that the program was not just for small companies. The best possibility was Charlie White and the Republic Steel Corporation. When we talked to Charlie White, George Dively said, "Charlie, I know you're worried about what your stockholders will think about this but I think stockholders are way ahead of us. I'll take the Harris Corporations annual meeting to any place in the country you specify and publicize it to show you that our shareholders will agree and not complain -- they'll actually applaud!" After some thought, Charlie White said, "No, George, you don't have to do that, I'll sign." And he did. And that was one of the keys to our success. We went on to get a group of 21 "initial" signers including Standard Oil of Ohio, and Xerox, and we decided to make an announcement nationally. (Joe Wilson of Xerox didn't want to "upstage" Eastman Kodak, which was the largest corporation in Rochester, so he wanted to be part of the "Cleveland Group.")

Fred Baker, who was head of corporate relations area at Harris Corporation, and I went to New York to visit the *New York Times* and talk to their editors. As a result, the *New York Times* wrote an editorial saying the Corporate 1% Program was one of the great steps forward in educational funding. At the same time an editorial appeared in the Los Angeles Times. Subsequently the *Readers' Digest* called me and sent one of their finest writers, Don Hall, to write a story which appeared in the *Readers' Digest*.

We then opened up a Corporate 1% office and hired a president to help promote the program to other cities in the country. Later we allied it with the Council for Financial Aid to Education in New York, which was a national organization devoted to higher education.

All the while I was still at Case.

George Dively suggested that I take a consulting fee for my work. I talked it over with the president of Case and he advised me to "ask enough." Also, Case and Western Reserve decided to merge and I became vice president of development of Case Western Reserve, a much larger institution.

In February of 1961, in the *Reader's Digest* and in newspapers and magazines across the country, the Corporate 1% Program for Higher Education was announced. Few plans in the history of philanthropy have been more widely heralded.

The *Reader's Digest* called the 1% Plan "America's Greatest Partnership..... Corporations and Colleges." *The New York Times* said editorially, "One of the most inventive and promising developments in meeting the problem of financing higher education – should spread far and wide." *The Los Angeles Times* called it, "A pioneering plan aimed at tripling the amount of money which U.S. corporations contribute to the nation's colleges and universities...A welcome partnership."

What these media were heralding was the decision of 21 Cleveland corporations to adopt a compact calling for "major increases in corporate contributions to higher education at once and increasing to a minimum of not less than one percent of income before taxes and thereafter gradually increasing as the need develops."

We felt an urgency in connection with higher education – not just the urgency of rapidly increasing enrollment – not just an urgency resulting from the threat of Russia or the threat of federal control. It was an urgency resulting from the fact that higher education was in jeopardy and that the future of our country depended upon our unique *dual* system.

"Everybody talks about doing something, but very few act," said Dively.

We decided to act!

The first action step was to put the "case" down on paper, concisely and clearly. Over the next several months, the "proposal to those who believe in American Leadership" emerged – a document ten paragraphs in length which stated our case.

"Our position among the nations of the world is being challenged," it began. "The showdown probably will come not in a test of arms but more likely in the race for supremacy in education and technology. At issue is the question whether or not our American Democracy *voluntarily*, can and will provide the necessary support to higher education."

In the middle was the 1% paragraph.

It ended, "we believe that the best interests of our country, our corporations, our stockholders and our employees will be served by this action. We are convinced that the time for practical, meaningful action is now!"

The next step was for the companies represented by the three co-chairmen to approve the proposal. This was done in subsequent months by placing the proposal and its 1% action paragraph before their boards.

Board approval then became one of the check-points of the program. In each case, the signing president or chairman of the board was asked specifically to get board approval for his action. For example, the Harris-Intertype Corporation board meeting minutes included the following paragraph, among others:

> The directors then discussed this proposal and unanimously concurred that the program was in the best interest of our company and that the company should endeavor to meet the objectives as set forth in the proposal.

We knew that we would need a "mix" of companies in order to have a meaningful leadership program from a national standpoint. We already had a billion-dollar sales corporation in Republic Steel, and two in the $50 million to $150 million category. We needed to fill the areas in between.

The initial group then set out to interest a small group of other Cleveland companies who were known to be uncommonly interested in higher education. At this time, we thought that a total of six companies (including the three initiators) would be sufficient for national leadership, so we invited eight companies to a luncheon meeting, explained the program and then proceeded to talk with them individually. We were elated when five of the eight signed up, including several companies in the $500 million range, and several in the "below $100 million" category. The new companies were TRW Inc., the Standard Oil Company (Ohio), the Hill Acme Company, the Warner & Swasey Company, and the Stouffer Corporation. We had the mix we were looking for.

And we had another bonus – we were beginning to get cross-fertilization among the boards.

Later, we held another confidential meeting at which we announced the action of the eight initial signers to approximately 50 other potential Cleveland signers. Following this meeting, and now using the eight initial signers as contact men, we signed up 13 more companies, all of them recognized as leaders in the Cleveland area and many also nationally known.

Then came the *Reader's Digest* story and the announcement of the program nationally.

The program began to have an impact on the entire nation.

John D. Rockefeller III, president of Rockefeller Foundation, had become interested in the program when he read *The New York Times* editorial and he wrote us at that time as follows:

> It has been a long time since I have read such heartening news in terms of American education and American business. Imagination and vision such as yours gives renewed confidence as to the future of our country.

Later, we asked him to speak at the annual meeting of the 1% group. When he came to Cleveland, he said:

> The members of the Cleveland 1% Compact have established themselves as practical pioneers, pointing and leading the way for others.
>
> I am most pleased to be here. And I think *you* should be most *proud* to be here. This is not said lightly. I truly believe that the work in which you are engaged – the common cause to which you stand committed – gives you a most serious reason for pride. For this is community action at its best – its most creative, constructive, and imaginative. It is also community action at its most *American*.
>
> You are, in fact, demonstrating leadership of the profoundest kind – beginning with the individual ... carrying through his business ... embracing his community, influencing both city and state ... and – in the final analysis – setting an example for our whole nation.

In 1968, we opened a national office for the 1% Program in Cleveland, and hardly a week went by which didn't bring some query from another section of the country interested in the 1% Program.

James C. Hardie

Kneeland Nunan was then named president and full time executive of the program. I remained as a paid consultant. The national office was supported by a $250,000 grant from the Ford Foundation and an equal amount from the 1% trustees and Cleveland 1% companies – mostly the trustees.

Naturally, we were proud of this accomplishment, but the corporations concerned also thought that it represented good business. Their contributions were gifts, but they were also investments.

If this program spread across the nation, and corporate giving could be increased to a minimum of 1%, $1 billion from corporations would be made available annually to higher education. (The level then was $380 million – 0.3%.)

What did the 1% Program produce in actual giving by the Cleveland companies? The first survey of the actual giving of the Cleveland signers was made in 1962 by the nationally known accounting firm, Ernst & Ernst. Results showed that the signers with a full year under the plan had reached an average of four-fifths of one percent of pre-tax income in annual gifts to higher education – more than double the national average of .3%.

Fifty Golden Years

Cleveland 1% Plan for Higher Education

YEAR	Corporate Contributions to Higher Education	Net Income of Companies Before Federal Income Taxes	Percent Contributions to Higher Education
1960	$1,726,127	$207,197,693	.83 %
1961	2,060,430	205,291,189	1.00
1962	2,325,738	213,647,517	1.09
1963	2,466,417	295,667,076	.83
1964	3,177,887	364,684,253	.87
1965	3,793,865	452,044,287	.84
1966	4,297,319	566,165,323	.76
1967	5,132,769	552,840,049	.93
1968	5,963,681	672,372,391	.89
1969	6,864,337	741,155,023	.93

Next, some other areas in the country became interested in the 1% Program, including Chattanooga, Tennessee, the first major 1% group outside of Cleveland.

Chattanooga then increased its number of signers to 29 corporations and conducted several annual surveys of giving. Then we announced a new 1% group in Knoxville, Tennessee, with 11 signers; a new program in Florida, with 10 signers; and one in California, with 16 signers. The California signers had taxable income in excess of $300 million.

Fifty Golden Years

Member Companies of the Corporate 1% Program for Higher Education, Inc.

CLEVELAND, OHIO
Organizing Chairman:
Jacob B. Perkins
American Greetings Corporation
Acme-Cleveland Corporation
API Instruments, Inc.
The Austin Company
Avery Engineering Company
Bardons & Oliver, Inc.
The Bodwell-Lemmon Company
The Coe Manufacturing Company
The Electric Furnace Company
The H.K. Ferguson Company
Ferro Corporation
The Griswold-Eshleman Company
Harris-Intertype Corporation
The Albert M. Higley Company
The Hill Acme Company
Hoag-Wismar-Henderson Associates
The Horsburgh & Scott Company
Hunkin-Conkey Construction Co.
Keithly Instruments, Inc.
W.O. Larson Foundry Company
Lord Corporation (Erie, PA)
The Lubrizol Corporation
Medusa Portland Cement Company
The Midland-Ross Corporation
Parker-Hannifin Corporation
Paterson-Leitch Company
The Penton Publishing Company
Pickands Mather & Co.
Republic Steel Corporation
The Sherwin-Williams Company

Sifco Industries, Inc.
The Standard Oil Company (Ohio)
The Stouffer Corporation
The Tremco Manufacturing Company
TRW Inc.
The Warner & Swasey Company
The Weatherhead Company
Work Wear Corporation
Xerox Corporation (Stamford, CT)
The Yoder Company

CALIFORNIA
Organizing Chairmen:
Arnold O. Beckman, Justin Dart,
and W. Parmer Fuller III
Avery Products, Incorporated
N.W. Ayer/Jorgensen/Macdonald Inc.
Beckman Instruments, Inc.
Brandow & Johnston Associates
Cubic Corporation
Cyprus Mines Corporation
Dart Industries, Inc.
Fluor Corporation, Ltd.
General Research Corporation
Hughes Aircraft Company
Industrial Indemnity Company
Scientific Data Systems, Inc.
Ralph C. Sutro Co.
Systems Technology, Inc.
Title Insurance & Trust Company

FLORIDA
Organizing Chairman: Philip J. Lee
Citizens National Bank of Orlando
Commercial Bank of Daytona Beach

James C. Hardie

First Bank & Trust Company
    of Boca Raton
First Federal Savings & Loan
Association of St. Petersburg
Hubbard Construction Company
Linder Industrial Machine Company
Charles MacArthur Dairies, Inc.
Publix Markets, Inc.
Radiation, Inc.
Milton Roy Company

Modern Apartments
Olan Mills Portrait Studios
Plymouth Laundry & Cleaners Co.
Purse Advertising
Red Food Stores
Rock City Gardens, Inc.
Stone Fort Land Company
W.C. Teas Company
Tennessee Paper Mills
Trotter, Boyd & Keese, Inc.
Trotter Pontiac Company

TENNESSEE - - CHATTANOOGA

Co-Chairmen: Howard B. Brooks, Sr., Will S. Keese, Olan Mills II, and William G. Raoul

Amos & Andy Buick Company
Brock Candy Company
Brooks Welding Supply Company
Business Music Company
Cavalier Corporation
Chattanooga Rubber Products
Chattanooga Times
Chattanooga Transfer & Storage
Chattem Drug & Chemical Company
Corley Manufacturing Company
Duff Brothers, Inc.
Forrest Cate Ford
Hailey Chevrolet Company
Hudson Printing & Lithographing Co.
Keese, Stephenson & Cambron, Inc.
Loveman's, Inc.
McKee Baking Company
Mills & Lupton Supply Company

- - KNOXVILLE

Chairman: John C. Bolinger, Jr.

Benco Plastics
Ceilheat, Inc.
Dealers Warehouse Corporation
Good and Goodstein, Architects
The Hassinger Organization
Knoxville Glove Company
Pilot Oil Corporation
K.W. Rogers & Son
Sheffield Steel Incorporated
Spinlab Inc.
Tennessee Metal Culvert

We subsequently merged the program into the CFAE and George Dively joined the CFAE board. I agreed to become a consultant to the CFAE. However, without the impetus of the Cleveland group, the program died a natural death, albeit a proud demise, with all participants realizing that they had significantly affected national gifts to higher education. At this time I was being asked to make talks all over the country about the 1% Program and the development advances in which I had participated. I received many awards and was forced to talk about myself and my background rather than give credit to others, which had been my long-time strict rule. The transition to "consultant" from college administrator was becoming almost seamless.

However, in retrospect, the "seamless growth" needs some documentation.

Not all Fred Crawford's influence was centered at Case Institute. Fred suggested that we add David Ingalls to the steering committee of the Western Reserve Historical Society Library Campaign, which we did. Dave was also on the steering committee of the first campaign I was connected with relative to the Museum of Natural History. That campaign leadership included Newt (Newman) Halvorson, who was one of the prominent, or perhaps the most prominent, member of the steering committee, although Boynton Murch was also very important. As mentioned before, Kent Smith was the major donor to that campaign, giving $4 million in matching gifts which was the key to the success of the campaign. Also, Boynton Murch made substantial gifts during the first phase of that campaign (we met in his office downtown) and when he thought that I was "struggling" a little bit, he would say, "Jim, I think you need another shot in the arm" and make a another substantial gift.

At the next campaign for the Museum of Natural History, David Ingalls "graduated" to a prime mover. (I think he was chairman of the board of the Museum at that time.) We worked together as a team and he functioned as the chairman throughout the campaign: In phase I (75% of the total), then phase II (20% of the total) and finally phase III (5% of the total). The numbers worked out perfectly.

Also, David became the principal leader in the Hawken campaign. He had received his early education there. We had a strong steering committee, but David was critical to the effort, which was successful. He would often say that we were "buddies," which was very unusual, but was an indication of how close we worked.

When David died from cancer, the entire philanthropic community lost one of its primary leaders.

It is also appropriate to mention that I had a relationship with David Ingalls, Sr., who I mentioned earlier was the first Naval Ace. David Jr. had such great respect for his father that when he knew about that earlier relationship, that seemed to be enough to warrant backing me 100% in any effort in which I was included. Many years before I got connected with David Jr. the senior Ingalls called me when I was vice president of CWRU and asked me about a "professorship" for Charles (Chick) Thomas, who was a doctor at University Hospitals. The senior Ingalls had a chronic eye problem which Dr. Thomas treated and the elder Ingalls wanted to reward Dr. Thomas with a named professorship. I explained that we didn't have endowed professorships for members of the University who had not died or retired and Mr. Ingalls said, "Jim, I'm sure you can work something out – hold it until Chick retires or whatever you want to do, but we'll work something out." I went down to his downtown office and when I got there he was ready with his special iced tea, which apparently he whipped up himself. I must admit it was some of the tastiest iced tea I've ever had. He asked me how much a professorship would cost and I said $500,000 (which was the official number at that time) and after we talked awhile he said, "I'm sure I can get that much; let me make some phone calls." He then proceeded to call various members of the Ingalls clan. Rather than ask them, he "told" them how much he proposed to take out of their assets. I'm not an expert on the Ingalls-Taft-Harkness relationship, but I know that Mrs. Ingalls made major gifts to Yale (she was a Harkness, which I think stems back to the Pennsylvania Railroad fortune). I knew of David Ingalls, Jr.'s relationship with the Tafts of Cincinnati because of his efforts to include me in the major political projects in which the Tafts were interested.

After Mr. Ingalls had completed his conversations, he said, "Jim, I wasn't able to get the entire $500,000, but I'm close to it and I'll get the rest of it very soon. I'll call upstairs and you can go up there and get the stock." And I said, "I don't think I should intervene in getting the actual stock – that might be more appropriate for one of our trustees." And he said, "No, I'd just like to complete this. You go upstairs and I'll tell them to give you the stock." So I went upstairs where there was a brokerage firm (I forget which one it was) and I walked out rather cautiously with a stack of stock which to my recollection was about twelve inches high.

Besides the Ingalls' interest in flying (both father and son) it is interesting to note, in looking back, how many of the men who were interested in philanthropy and the top institutions in Cleveland were also interested in flying. I've already mentioned Fred Crawford's part in starting the air races in Cleveland, and Ray Livingston, the vice president for human relations at TRW, was also a pilot, and I think the first man to fly across Lake Erie; David Swetland, who I mentioned before, was also a pilot and flew his own plane up until the time he was 80; Bill Mattie, the president of Eaton whom I've mentioned and who we enlisted as the Phase II chairman of the $17,250,000 St. Luke's campaign, was also a pilot; Walter Sparling, the president of Ohio Bell, was a pilot and he told me he was enlisted from his family's front porch to become a British pilot before World War II. Also, Kent Smith, who has been prominently mentioned throughout this philanthropic book, also had his own plane and was a pilot. Later Kent flew one of the Lubrizol planes out of the Lost Nation Airport, which is east of Cleveland, and told me that he gave up flying when he went out to get his plane, which was one of several planes that Lubrizol had in a hangar at Lost Nation, where they had the finest available mechanical care. When he took off and flew several miles, to his dismay he noted that the gas tank was empty! He turned around and just made is back to Lost Nation. They had forgotten to gas up the plane! After that, Kent gave up flying. Also, Jim Dunlap, who took up flying after retiring from a top executive position at TRW, learned to fly and made several long solo trips which were well publicized. He became chairman of the

Ohio Presbyterian Retirement Campaign where I was the consultant. Maybe "Risk Takers" become successful philanthropists!

During all of the many philanthropic efforts in Cleveland, especially at VGS (Vocational Guidance and Rehabilitation Center Services) and the Museum of Natural History, Bob Gries always seemed to be in the background. He also asked me to take a look at consulting at the Cleveland Ballet, where Bob was an important leader, but in a very rare situation, I took a hard look and came to the conclusion that the Ballet didn't have the type of board leadership that would allow them to be successful in the long-run.

I'm sorry to say that my judgment proved to be correct. But the Ballet did continue to be an important institution in Cleveland for at least 30 years before it went out of business and did bring a lot of joy to thousands of Clevelanders before it failed. It's very interesting to note that after Vincent Smith died, his second wife became a very important contributor to the Ballet. The fact that the Cleveland Ballet held on for so many years was the result of many last minute injections of funds, not the least of which were injections by Mrs. Vincent Smith.

An interesting note on Bob Gries is that early in my career (probably in the 60's) Bob Gries took an interest in my theory that in order to be successful, 75% of the money in a capital campaign must come from the top 100 givers. He called me and said that for many years (20 or so) he had been checking out my theory and always found that I was right. But the call concerned a Yale campaign (Bob is a Yale graduate) and he had checked it out and said he thought that he had finally found one campaign where I was wrong. But he said he wanted to make sure that he had the right statistics before he called me and said he checked with Yale and found that I was still right. The reason for the potential discrepancy was that Yale had added all of the funds from their annual giving during the years of the campaign, and when you subtracted those annual funds, 75% of the capital campaign still came from the top 100 givers.

Art Holden refused to take a "titled" position in major philanthropic efforts, but during my entire career, he seemed to be on the edges of many of the things I did. Art was from Painesville,

James C. Hardie

245 Springdale Lane ▪ Chagrin Falls, Ohio 44022
216 / 831-2488

With compliments of the author.

graduated from Case around 1932, and has been connected with Case and the Cleveland Clinic for many, many years. Early in my career, he asked me to be a consultant and conduct a major campaign for Morley Library in Painesville. I said I couldn't do it because they didn't have a development officer that I could work with because the library was so small. But Art, who was known to be a person who couldn't take "no" as an answer, said that he would call our friend Al Pike, who was chairman at that time of the Painesville National Bank, to get someone from the bank who could serve as a development officer. They eventually recruited the wife of one of the top executives of the bank. She called and told me that she knew nothing about development and really had no great skills but if I told her what to do, she would do it. With great trepidation, I agreed to give it a try and as I look back, I don't know how we did it, but the campaign was successful.

Art was supportive to the Lake County Y campaign and gave, behind the scenes, support to the Holden Arboretum Campaign. (He always said that the Holden name of the Arboretum was not from his family, but I'm not so sure of that.)

In connection with the Holden Arboretum campaign, I agreed to help train Molly Offett, the daughter of the McMillen-Mather family. Molly, who never took credit for the great job she did, turned out to be one of the best development persons I helped spawn.

Art Holden was also helpful behind the scenes in the Breckenridge Retirement Center Campaign. I remember that he arranged behind the scenes for a very fine gift from the Reinberger Foundation.

When I was a consultant at the Ohio College of Podiatric Medicine, I helped arrange a special award, the first of which was given to Art. It was a sculpture by Bill McVey, the great Cleveland architect, of a bushel basket held up by an angled stake and illuminated with a candle which indicated that recipients hid their talents and good deeds under a bushel basket. Art certainly met those qualifications.

I should also mention Theo Moll who was a tremendously successful executive who immigrated from Germany to this country as a tool and die maker. Though he could not speak English, he communicated with the foreman of his group when he needed a new tool or some help through another worker who spoke both German and English. Bill Mattie, the president of Eaton, was very close to Theo because he helped him start his own business, MTD Products. He told me why Theo started the business. He said that, one day, Theo needed a tool and went over to his translator and said he needed a tool and the fellow-worker said just go up and tell him (the foreman) that he's "a son of a bitch." Theo did and the foreman punched him in the mouth. Bill said that Theo made up his mind at that moment that he was never going to work for anybody again. So he started down the path of founding MTD Products with Bill Mattie's help. In due course, MTD Products became very successful and Theo, who was a staunch Methodist, decided to help found the Cleveland Mission, which was a carry-over from his father who had an interest in a small mission in Germany.

I got to know Theo through Bill Mattie when Bill agreed to help us solicit Theo in the original St. Luke's $17,250,000 campaign. Later, Theo was interested in the Salvation Army when I was a consultant in that campaign, and much later in the Elyria Methodist Home Campaign where I was the consultant. My recollection was that in the Elyria campaign, Theo gave $250,000. When we asked him how he arrived at that figure, he said that he "prayed and that figure came to him." Later we had a high-level meeting of possible potential steering committee members in connection with the campaign, and as we were sitting around a small table (I guess that there were ten or twelve of us) Theo said, "Jim, why am I here?" And I answered, "Theo, everyone else here is asking the same question but they look over and see you and they know how generous you are and they'll think, "If Theo is here, I guess it's okay."

For some reason or other (perhaps in connection with the Fairview Hospital campaign where I was a consultant) I visited Theo at his plant on the west side of Cleveland. He immediately took me out in the back of the plant and showed me a beautiful stand of pine trees and very proudly told me that when he built that plant, he had planted those trees and now they were grown and beautiful for him to see out of his office window. Since I grow trees as a hobby, I understood his pride.

As written otherwise in this book, Theo was also interested in the west side portion of the YMCA campaign when I was a consultant to the Y. When I wanted to meet with Theo, he wouldn't have lunch with me at the Union Club because that was "too far east." He preferred to meet at the Clifton Club which was on the west side.

Stan Pace was one of "Fred Crawford's boys" who became vice chairman of TRW and later went on to St. Louis and became chairman of General Dynamics. My path crossed with Stan's many times because he was interested in education and became a member of the Orange School Board before I did. Later he became chairman of the Shaker Heights School Board.

When I became a consultant to Judson Retirement Center, I looked over the list of residents of Judson and noted that Stan's mother-in-law was a resident there. Since we were looking ahead to a capital campaign at Judson, I had recommended that we make a strong effort to add prominent people to the board. I then recommended that they ask Stan Pace to become a member of the board. They didn't think they had any chance of getting him, but using the best persuasion I could mount, I got them to ask him and he immediately turned them down saying he was much too busy.

The day they asked him and he turned them down, he called me at home at night and said, "Jim, I assume you're behind this push to get me on the Judson board." And I said, "Stan, I plead guilty." He said, "Well what do you want me to do?" I said, "Stan, the board needs to be substantially strengthened and I think that you could do that if you become chairman of the nominating committee." He said, "I turned them down and when I got home, my wife said, 'Stan you can help everybody in the country, but you can't help your mother-in-law.' I'll do it, Jim, so just tell me some of the people you want to get and I'll go out and try to get them." He did and this proved to be one of the pivotal points in the development of Judson.

Later, I was a consultant to Wade Park Manor, which also was a retirement home. It got into financial trouble because it lacked a nursing home.

I suggested that Wade Park Manor and Judson Park merge, which would give Wade Park access to Judson's nursing home and would make the combined entity a brilliant star in the University Circle area.

Anyone who has ever tried to merge two institutions knows the great number of emotional issues involved, and this proposed merger had as many issues as most mergers.

I was not making much headway in selling the idea when Stan Pace said, "I believe Jim is right. I think that this merger would be good for both institutions, but more so, I think it would be good for Cleveland." His support won the day and although I count this as one of my favorite accomplishments, I know it would not have been done without the support and the help and stature of Stan Pace.

While I was a consultant at Lake Erie College, after the Equestrian Center campaign was a success, I talked with President Paul Weaver who told me that he had a call from one of the two Reinberger brothers who said that his daughter was a student in the Lake Erie College Equestrian program and that they'd like to talk about helping out. Paul had no idea who they were or what kind of resources they had. But I knew, because of my research, that their uncle, who had started one of the big auto parts businesses in the country and lived in Columbus, had died and there were rumors that quite a large foundation to be called The Reinberger Foundation was being set up. I told Paul and he said maybe he could ask them for $5,000 to help pave the area around the new Equestrian Center, which was a mess. He called me a couple of weeks later and said, "Jim, they not only said they would give $5,000 toward the paving around the Center but they would pave the entire area."

This was my introduction to the Reinberger brothers who have since given millions of dollars in the Cleveland area and take a salary for running the foundation of only $10,000 each per year.

Incidentally, both of the Reinberger brothers, Robert and William, are engineers; one worked at TRW until he retired and the other worked at the NASA until he retired.

I asked Fred Crawford to intercede for a gift to the Historical Society and he did and they made a handsome gift. The scuttlebutt was that they didn't like the fact that Fred interceded because they thought that they could not say "no" to him. But during my career I can remember major gifts from the Reinbergers to the Institute of Music, the Museum of Natural History, Lake Erie College, the Cleveland Playhouse, and many more.

Tom Taylor, Sr. was a remarkable man and one of the greatest salesmen I have ever met. He volunteered at St. Luke's Hospital and was on the board and the development committee. He told me that when he was in college (I think a freshman at Ohio Wesleyan) he got a summer job with a contractor who was building houses and hired Tom to sell them. Tom did so well that he never returned to college. He later started National Machinery and built it into a very profitable company. He also was very kind to elderly widows, often "squiring" them to dinners and other affairs. We asked him to chair a bequest and deferred gifts program, which was the first bequest program in Cleveland other than the Case effort. We set a goal of getting 100 friends of St. Luke's to put St. Luke's in their wills or make a deferred gift to St. Luke's. We did this over a period of time and reported the numbers as they climbed toward 100. The development committee of St. Luke's helped Tom, but a substantial portion of the program's success was due to Tom Taylor. When we reached 100, we then decided to continue to work to keep the number at 100 as the various bequests were received and we were successful. I know of no other bequest program in Cleveland which equaled the St. Luke's program headed by Tom Taylor.

Maury Struchen was climbing the ladder in the banking business at the same time I was climbing the ladder at Case. He started out at National City Bank and then switched over to Society National Bank and finally became chairman of Society Bank (Fred Crawford was on the board at Society). Along the way, Maury talked to me about a boys camp that his dad was interested in and asked that I give him some pointers on how his dad could raise money for the camp. I did.

Later, Maury was on the steering committee of the campaign for the Elyria United Methodist Home where I was a consultant and became one of the "stars" of that campaign.

He told me some wonderful stories about how he became so successful in the banking business. He said that he came back to Cleveland after getting an advanced degree and was walking down Euclid Avenue and stopped at the National City Bank to ask one of the executives there for a job. He said the executive talked to him for a while and finally said, "Maury, do you tithe?" And Maury said, "No, I don't." And the executive said, "Maury, if you decide that you're going to tithe, I'll give you a job and pay you 'X amount of dollars.'" Maury said that he had just come back to Cleveland, that he and his wife had a new baby, and he would go home and talk it over. They did talk it over and he told the executive that they would tithe immediately after the first year of his employment.

Maury said that they kept their promise, and they started to tithe (give ten percent of their salary to charity). He said that was the most important decision that he had made in his career.

I am certain that the contacts he made because of the tithing and all the other ramifications of that kind of leadership giving, brought him lasting respect. Also, other executives at Society Bank took leadership in philanthropic efforts because it became "company policy" to volunteer.

During my early career in Cleveland, I didn't have much connection with Herb Strawbridge. He was a protégé of the head of Higbee's, John Murphy, and became a power in philanthropy after John Murphy died. He later became head of the Murphy Foundation and was very important in Cleveland philanthropy because of the gifts from the Murphy Foundation.

He also became the driving force behind the Health Museum in the 80's and '90's. He was not connected with the Health Museum when I was a consultant during the time when Lowell Bernard was the executive director.

I think that Herb Strawbridge was responsible for separating Lowelll Bernard, who didn't get along with many board members, from the Health Museum and bringing on the new director, Michael Marks.

I worked with Herb on the Regina Health Center Campaign where he was very helpful, and on the Ursuline College Campaign where he chaired the campaign steering committee and was also chairman of the Ursuline board. We conducted a successful campaign to build a library in honor of Ralph Besse, who was most responsible for moving Ursuline from University Circle to Pepper Pike.

One of the most interesting stories that Herb told me about his background concerned his education at Purdue University. He went to Purdue University from a farm high school and decided to take an engineering course. He quickly learned he didn't have the mathematics background to study engineering.

Somehow he got a copy of the charter for Purdue University and read that the dean of the Engineering School had the right to start a business school. So Herb set about trying to convince the dean that he should start a business school with Herb as its first student. The dean was very reluctant, of course, but after quite a bit of maneuvering by Herb, agreed to do so and allow Herb to be the first student. Thus, Herb said, he became the first graduate of the Purdue Business School, which is now one of the premiere business schools in the nation.

Herb was also interested in VGS, and when I became consultant to VGS, he was one of the first people I talked with. Higbee's had a restaurant and Herb said that some of the best employees that he had were people trained at VGS. He said that because they were handicapped and many had never had a job which paid them for their services, they made great employees. They did their jobs very conscientiously, had great attitudes toward the customers, reported on time, and were very happy with what they were doing.

Herb told me an interesting story about Harvard MBA's who were considered, at that time, to be the future corporate leaders of the nation. After they graduated, Harvard would send them around the country to talk with leading business people.

One time, Herb was asked to talk with three Harvard MBA's and he agreed to do so, and took them to lunch. While they were at lunch, he proposed an interesting question to all three. Herb said to the three graduate students, "Higbee's just concluded its fiscal year and we have ascertained how much profit we made during the year." He asked, "How much of this profit should we give to charity?" The first graduate student said that he thought Higbee's ought to give fifteen percent of their profit to charity. The second said he thought they should give thirty percent. The third said he thought they ought to give fifty percent. Herb's point in telling the story was that here were three graduate students from one of the leading universities in the country who were going out to become potential business leaders and they obviously didn't have a clue relative to the philanthropic area.

I got to know Henry Norweb when I was a consultant to the Holden Arboretum during the time that Henry was its director. It is well known that the Norwebs were among the most important "society" leaders of Cleveland. Certainly, Henry's mother, Emory Mae Norweb, was one of the most powerful forces in Cleveland's upper echelons. Although he was not a powerful force in downtown Cleveland, I found that Henry had the type of connections necessary to do the kind of work that leads towards success in major campaigns. I enjoyed working with him and observing his "laid back" style. During the time I was a consultant to the Cleveland Council of World Affairs, we worked out an endowment naming the Council's Executive Director's "Chair" in honor of Henry's father (who had been an ambassador). When Henry died prematurely from a fall at his summer home in Maine, the community suffered a great loss.

I don't want to leave the impression that all the philanthropic leadership in the Golden Years was male, for it was not. Among all the women who do yeomen work in the philanthropic area, I would place Sue Harrison near the top of the list. Sue is remarkably organized and is personally oriented, a volunteer who does the best job of following up, saying "thank you," and remembering what she said she would do, of anybody I ever met. She was the wife of Stu Harrison, who played a major part in the development of the Cleveland Foundation. She has a fine relationship with the top people in Cleveland. She is also articulate and has a great sense of humor. It was her leadership that made the Beechbrook campaign a success. One incident in connection with that campaign occurred when we were not certain that any corporation would give to the Beechbrook campaign because it was a small institution which treated emotionally disturbed children. We thought the corporations would demur. We looked for a way to break the log jam and get one of the corporations to make a gift in the hope that others would follow. Stu Harrison was chairman of Cleveland Cliffs and when our proposal came before the board of Cleveland Cliffs, Stu Harrison recused himself and said the board would have to decide because he certainly was biased. Then Colin Baldwin, who was on the board and chairman of Sherwin Williams Company, made an impassioned speech saying that all of us know how difficult it is to get someone to agree to be the chairman of a campaign and he felt that companies should try to support people who took that kind of leadership, whether they were the wife of the chairman or not. He made the motion to approve the gift. It passed!

As an example of Sue's leadership, Severance Millikan made an early gift to the Beechbrook Campaign of (in my recollection) $50,000 and at the Union Club one day, took me aside and said, "Jim, I don't agree with that campaign you're running for Beechbrook. Far too much money is spent on each of those children. The money would be more profitably spent in other ways." And I said, "Severance, I know that you gave $50,000. Feeling the way you do, why did you do it?" And he sheepishly said, "I couldn't figure out any way to say no to Sue!"

Sue also took leadership in getting a matching gift from the Kresge Foundation for Beechbrook, which certainly must go down as one of the longest shots in history. She did it by calling on several personal contacts who had ties to members of the Kresge board.

Sue also took leadership at Judson Park – Wade Park Manor, and in the second phase of the campaign for Laurel School. Although Sue is well into her 80's, she continues to function as one of the "stem-winders" of philanthropy in Cleveland.

Elizabeth Chamberlain was the major reason for the success of the Cleveland Garden Center Campaign (now the Botanical Garden). Elizabeth always said to me, as we continued to progress towards success in the Garden Center Campaign, "Jim, I don't know how you do it." And my answer always was, "Elizabeth, I'm not doing it, you're doing it." And she was, yet she was sincere in crediting me for our success. And the only way I can figure it out is I controlled when we did certain things, how much we asked for in certain instances, and how things should be prepared in order to make the volunteers successful. But from my standpoint, nothing would have happened to the Garden Center without the leadership of Elizabeth Chamberlain and her stature in the community.

Sister Marthe Rinehart also, in my opinion, ranks right near the top of the wonderful women in philanthropy in Cleveland. I first met her when she was president of Notre Dame College in Cleveland, and we conducted a very successful capital campaign for the college.

I wasn't the only one who recognized Sister Marthe's unusual talents. Bob Ginn, who was then chairman of Cleveland Electric Illuminating Company, where Sister Marthe was on the board (this too was unusual at that time) said to me that even though he had some of the top leaders of other corporations on the CEI board, Sister Marthe was the best board member he had. She has a remarkable talent for cutting to the heart of a problem and articulating what should be done about it. She later became director of development for the Sisters of Notre Dame at their 600 acre mother house and school, east of Cleveland in Geauga County.

Later, she asked me to be a consultant to try to merge the school, which was called Notre Dame, together with the remnants of Cathedral Latin School which had closed down (it had been in Cleveland) but still had a remarkably successful alumni group. We were successful in merging the schools although there were political problems as well as the usual problems of raising a significant sum of money. There is no doubt that without the leadership of Sister Marthe, it would never have been done. Notre Dame Cathedral Latin School is now a successful enterprise.

Donna Reid was chairman of the board of Laurel School when I was a consultant there. She was a dynamic leader. She also at the time was, as I remember, the head of The Center for Alcoholism in Cleveland and worked full-time, although it was obvious she didn't need to. We conducted a very successful campaign for Laurel School when very few capital campaigns were conducted for girls' schools.

Early in the campaign when I outlined my method of "evaluation," Donna Reid said there's no way that anybody's going to tell us (the Reids) what to give, "We've already made up our minds and we're going to give $25,000." I said, "Nevertheless, we should go on with the evaluation," and we did. We soon came to a couple that Donna Reid said were very good friends of the Reids and she said, "I think, if properly asked, they could give $50,000."

We ultimately concluded the evaluation and started the first solicitations.

At the first meeting when we were reporting our initial efforts, Donna Reid said that she had good news and that she had asked her friends who were evaluated at $50,000, and they had agreed! She added, "Now we have two gifts for $50,000." I said, "Donna, who are the second $50,000 givers?" And she said, "Oh, it's us." And I said, "Donna, I thought you said you were not going to give any more than $25,000." She said, "Well, we have as much money as they have, and if they were going to give $50,000 there is no way we could give less!"

I've tried to cover some of the women who had pivotal influence in the success of the many major campaigns and institutions with which I was connected. I am certain that there might be criticism of my choice of the women who have done yeomen service to philanthropy during the 50 Golden Years of Philanthropy, and the criticism would be justified. In other sections of the book I have mentioned Martha Joseph, who certainly is one of the "wonderful" women because of her work at the Institute of Music and other institutions. Lindsay Morgenthaler certainly would be near the top of the heap because of her tremendous organizational ability and because of the many successful special events which she has chaired. She also qualifies as a philanthropist in her own right.

Jim Biggar was connected with Fred Crawford because of the aforementioned relationship between Gordon Stouffer and the Stouffer Corporation and Fred. Jim Biggar married Marjorie Stouffer and became a force in the Stouffer Corporation. He climbed to the top of the Stouffer Corporation and after the merger with Nestle he became the top person in Nestle USA. I knew him because he was a Case alumnus and we ran against each other for the Orange Board of Education. We both were elected and that started a rather long relationship.

Jim was also interested in the Vocational Guidance Center where I was a consultant for 20 years, and our paths crossed there many times. When I was asked to consult for the "New Cleveland Campaign," Jim was chairman of the steering committee. Without a doubt, he was the single most important factor in the success of that campaign.

Another "behind the scenes" important philanthropist was Fred Lennon who had a small but profitable engineering company, Swagelok, while I was at Case. He made annual gifts to Case and that's how I got to know him. He later became one of the wealthiest men in Cleveland with more than a billion dollars.

Early in my consulting career he called and asked me to be a consultant to a small Catholic retirement home on Lander Road in a suburb of Cleveland called "The Home of the Divine Redeemer." He told me I should work with a very bright Ph.D., Sister Henrietta, who had just become connected with the home. He said, "Send her out to see Hugh O'Neill and I think he'll give $100,000 and I'll give $100,000 and then we ought to be able to get enough money to take care of those staff sisters who are getting up in years. Most of the people in the retirement home have died and we have to take care of the sisters. "

While we were doing this, he said to me, "Jim, you WASPs have all the money so I've got to take care of the Catholics." I said, "Fred, that isn't true, you know I cover the entire philanthropic field and I can tell you that the Irish Catholics have substantial wealth and are second to no one."

In the ensuing years there was no doubt that Fred Lennon became a major force in Catholic philanthropy in Cleveland, along with the O'Neills, as well as the entire philanthropic area.

Jacob B. "Tim" Perkins was a gem. He was one of my favorite people. Although he was president of a smaller company, Hill Acme, his impact along the way in the Fifty Golden Years went far beyond the size of his company. The chairman of the board of Hill Acme, A. C. McDaniel, was the second signer of the Corporate 1% Program for Higher Education. Tim became the chairman of the company and at one point became co-chairman of the Corporate 1% Program. The 1% group honored Tim in October, 1979 and presented him with a silver tray including the etched signatures of all the other signers. At that time he wrote me a handwritten letter which said, "The recognition and beautiful tray will stay a warm and proud event in my life as long as I am around." His letter then continued, "Working with you over these many years has been one of the happiest experiences in my life. Your enthusiasm, knowledge, and sound judgment to make other people have a better life is inspiring."

The Perkins family had major historical ties to the Cleveland area. Edgewater Park was originally the Perkins family farm and the Grandfather O'Neal, the scion of the O'Neal family which founded Leaseway Trucking Company, was originally the Perkins family coachman and the great Leaseway Company grew out of that experience.

At a party, I introduced Tim to one of the younger O'Neals, and it was evident that although they had never met, the respect that the young O'Neal paid Tim Perkins and the respect that Tim showed in return indicated that the relationship of the two families was exemplary.

Tim's half-brother, Leigh, spent much of his time away from Cleveland and founded Orvis Company, which is now nationally, or perhaps even internationally, known and is located in Vermont.

I remember a letter I treasure is a handwritten one from Tim at the time of my mother's death in 1972. He wrote, "I know you had a great mother." That simple sentence touched my heart because it was true. I once said to Tim, "You are one of the most gracious and kind people I have ever met. I know you were born with a silver spoon in your mouth, so how did your parents influence you when you were young?" He said, "My dad always said that I would have a place to sleep and something to eat, but beyond that I'd have to make my own way. I guess I was dumb enough to believe him!"

Sadly, Tim had Alzheimer's late in his life and went into a nursing home. When I asked about visiting him, his family said that they would have to fill him in on who I was and what our relationship was because he would remember none of it. But I have the joy of remembering Tim, one of Cleveland's finest.

Although I've mentioned Jim Hodge several times in other parts of this overview, I think Jim Hodge merits more attention. He was very important to the Salvation Army in Cleveland and served on the Salvation Army board. He was also a very successful scholar in metallurgy and was one of the two people in Cleveland who received the Sever Award from the American Society of Metals. Jim became chairman of Warner and Swazey after Walter Bailey. Jim was also a trustee at Case and a graduate of Case. He was able to attend Case because of the scholarship he received in the 20's. He was a great gin rummy player and several of his buddies told me the story about the time they decided to take the ship that goes up along the Alaskan coast to look at the glaciers. They said most of the time they sat in one of the lounges in the middle of the ship and played gin rummy. Of course everybody was waiting for a sight of the glaciers and when they were sighted there was quite a lot of excitement and most people rushed to the rails of the ship where they could see the glaciers. They said that Jim looked up from his gin rummy hand for a moment and then looked down and said, "Let's get on with the game."

Walter Bailey was very much interested in Oberlin College. In fact he was one of the older graduates of Oberlin, and at times when I marched in their commencement exercises (I was representing

Case) I teamed up with Walter Bailey. But the point is that Warner and Swazey had leadership which was very much interested in higher education and the records show that many, many times made leadership gifts that got the ball rolling in major campaigns.

Toward the end of his life, Jim Hodge was looking for a place where he could comfortably live rather than in the big house that he and his wife owned in University Heights. When his wife died, he approached me with a unique proposition: He knew about the area that we live in, Moreland Hills, because he had tried to buy a house (I think it was for his son-in-law), which is in an area not too far from our place. We have almost five acres, which abut the valley leading down to the Chagrin River. Part of the property is a very beautiful two-acre plot which is nicely treed and overlooks the ravine which leads down to the aforementioned valley. And somehow, Jim learned that I owned this piece of property and offered to build a small house on it that he could live out his life in, and then bequeath it to me. I let the request by Jim die a natural death because I knew he had two lovely daughters who were adults and I just didn't want to get entwined with his estate. I still feel a little guilty about it.

I have mentioned Alex Nason in a number of sections of this book, but I think he merits individual attention. As I've written before, Kelvin Smith told me that Alex was "everything" in those early days of Lubrizol. He was a great salesman and a very interesting guy. His wife, "Bakey," had a stroke when Alex was chairman of Lubrizol and Alex decided to devote his life to her. He personally taught her to talk and regain many of her previous abilities. He spent hours reading to her. I gave them a gift of Bronowski's *Ascent of Man* and Alex told me how much they enjoyed reading the book together. I remember a story of Alex's tenacity that John Baird, his best friend, told me. A group of Lubrizol people, including Alex, were in a bar and someone suggested that they try to throw a dime into a bottle cap from about ten feet. After quite a bit of time, most of the participants gave up and left, but John said that Alex persisted until finally he was able to do it.

Alex had a home in Nassau in the Bahamas and invited Em and me down to that area and arranged for us to stay at Lyford

Cay. On the day that we were going to fly to Nassau, there was a tremendous blizzard in Cleveland and we had to check into a hotel near the airport. Alex sent a telegram saying that he called and found out our new time of arrival and when we got to Nassau, he was there to greet us.

Lyford Cay is a beautiful and exclusive resort that caters to wealthy international types with huge yachts. It has a beautiful golf course and exquisite food. Alex had also invited Kelvin and Eleanor Smith to be his guests and we were pleased to be able to meet with them while we were there.

Alex brought us a bag of cookies, which he had baked, and told us that for years he had been baking cookies and giving them to special friends. But I have an addendum to the story which is that they were the most awful cookies I've ever eaten. I guess nobody ever had the guts to tell kind and wonderful Alex that he was not a baker.

When Liv Ireland, who had a sizeable yacht, heard that we had been to Lyford Cay, he said (a joke) that Lyford Cay was one of those exclusive places where you couldn't hang your underwear out to dry on your yacht's yardarm."

Toward the end of their lives, Alex and Bakey moved out to the Breckenridge Presbyterian Home and lived in two cottages on that property. Just before he died, Alex gave $1 million to Breckenridge toward a nursing home, which they didn't have. I was pleased to be asked to be the consultant on that campaign, which was successful and funded the Alex Nason Nursing Home. An interesting sidelight on that campaign is that a substantial portion (more than $1 million to my recollection) was contributed to that campaign by the people who were retired and living in the Presbyterian Home.

Jack Reavis was the Managing Partner of Jones, Day, Cockley, and another Case trustee who was a Crawford admirer and very influential in the early Golden Years. During the sixties, when there were so many hostile takeovers of corporations, I was in my office one day with Jack Reavis and a call came in for him and he decided to take it and told me that I need not give him any privacy. It was soon evident that the caller was the chairman of a major corporation who was asking Jack Reavis to be the lawyer in some litigation involving a takeover of his company. Jack listened for awhile and said, "I appreciate your asking me to represent you but I can't do it because I'm going to be representing the other corporation and I want to tell you now, I'm going to kick your ass every chance I get." He was a no-nonsense type of guy and had what I thought to be one of the more brilliant minds in Cleveland. He didn't seem to do much socially and usually had lunch most days alone at the Mid-Day Club in Cleveland.

He was the trustee designated to be an advisor to me when needed and since he was so busy he assigned Art Dougan one of their top lawyers to also serve in that capacity because it was evident that Jack would not be available at times.

When Jack was available, there was no doubt that he was tremendously important to Case.

To illustrate Jack's importance, there was and is a major foundation in Cleveland called the Kulas Foundation which was dedicated to support, in the main, "music," and Jack Reavis and his firm were the Kulas lawyers.

Because Kulas was dedicated to making gifts to "music," everyone assumed that they would not make a gift to an engineering school such as Case. But I decided to talk to Jack Reavis about it and I told him that we certainly could use the funds if there was any way he could figure out to have the Kulas Foundation make a gift to Case.

He thought about it for a while and said, "You know, I haven't been over to see Mrs. Kulas in some time, so I'll get a bottle of wine and go over and see her."

We subsequently wrote a proposal for $100,000 and gave it to Jack who did as he said he would. It came as a surprise to everyone when the Kulas Foundation gave us the $100,000. It was all because of Jack, and again proved how important the personal approach is.

On one issue concerning the Sam Emerson Construction Company I turned to Jack. It was a time when the construction business was down and we were building several new buildings on the Case campus. The construction details were handled by the physical plant department, but I was relied on because the support of the bidders was an important part of the decision. The Sam Emerson Company was one of the most important contractors because Sam was a graduate of Case, and had been a star on the Case football team. In addition, even though he was known as "Silent Sam," he was one of our finest trustees and certainly one of the finest men I've ever met.

When Keith Glennan became president of Case, Sam Emerson was chairman of the board. Keith told me later that Sam taught him an important lesson. Apparently, a very important issue was facing Case and Glennan was having a problem deciding what to do about it. So he phoned Sam and told him about the problem and said, "Sam, what do you think I should do?" Keith told me there was a long pause (he said it was probably about five seconds but it seemed like 30 seconds to him) and then Sam quietly said, "Keith, it isn't important what I think should be done, what are you going to do?" Keith told me he never made that mistake again.

Sam came to me later and said, "Jim, the construction business is way down and our company is also way down. I know that you take three bids on all major construction but I want you to know that I need to get the contract for the "X" building." (I forget which building it was.) And, he continued, "I know your policy on bidding is fair and just, but if you give me the contract for the "X" building I will give Case the Sam Emerson Construction Company."

I immediately realized that this was a major issue. The Albert W. Higley Construction Company was run by Ab Higley, who was also a Case graduate, but not a trustee. Ab undoubtedly would be bidding for the building.

I called Jack Reavis and arranged for him to be present when I would discuss this offer with Sam Emerson.

The three of us met in the president's office (the president was not there), to talk about the gift.

I learned very quickly why Jack Reavis was one of the nation's premium lawyers. Although Reavis and Emerson were both trustees of Case and obviously had known each other for a long

Fifty Golden Years

time, Jack Reavis was as tough and pragmatic in that situation as I could conceive, actually to the point where I was embarrassed. He drew up a contract with Sam which spelled out specifically how and under what terms the Sam Emerson Company would become an asset of Case.

To complete this story, Case owned the company for several years and later the top employees of the company bought it back from Case.

During my career I have met many important and interesting people who I didn't know long enough or intimately enough to cover more thoroughly, but they left a major impression. One of them, whom I call "Stars," was Ansel Adams, the internationally known and acclaimed photographer. I met him while I was a consultant to the University of Rochester for their $10 million campaign. Eastman Kodak[1] was very interested in the University of Rochester and said that if we planned to produce a brochure for the campaign, they were paying Ansel Adams $1,000 a day to do some work for Kodak and they would be glad to lend him to us for the brochure. Of course this was a tremendous "ten-strike" and I proceeded to lay out a brochure and began to oversee the preparation of the copy.

I then met with Ansel Adams and we decided to take photos of some of the faculty and some important views of the university, which is very beautiful.

---

[1] Fred Crawford had been a board member of Eastman Kodak, and we talked many times about the company. Fred had a great admiration for Kodak and he once said to me, "Go into your favorite drugstore in your mind and take a look behind the counter and what do you see?" Of course, the answer was, "Those little yellow boxes."

There always has been some difference of opinion between Cleveland and Rochester, New York, about who started the Community Chest. I'm sure that is well documented somewhere in the historical files. But there is an interesting story that I picked up while I was in Rochester as a consultant to the University of Rochester. The leaders there said that George Eastman was not one to fail in an endeavor he was connected with and that during the first Community Chest in Rochester (the historical files will indicate what these efforts were actually called) George Eastman took a full page ad in The Rochester Times that said, "These people and corporations have refused to give to the Community Chest," and he actually listed those who had declined.

93

James C. Hardie

Adams was a very interesting person who was known as a "purist photographer." He used a box camera and developed his own pictures, unlike Margaret Bourke White, a Clevelander who took a hundred photos so you could choose ten or fifteen that you wanted to use. Adams asked me how many pictures I wanted. When I said 17, he said, "Well, then we'll take 18."

When we had the kind of picture set up that we wanted, he would call me over to the big box camera and say, "Jim, take a look what we have there, because that's what you're going to get." He was really a genius. He would compose a picture with a glint of light on a leaf in the right-hand corner, and another glint on the left-hand corner, and overall it would look like an impressionist composition. I could write an entire chapter on some of the techniques he used, but I'll mention just one to indicate the brilliance of Adams.

We wanted to use a striking picture as the end of the brochure and that would give any alumnus the "feeling" of the University of Rochester. To do this, we found a small hill above a field where there was a very beautiful tree standing alone. Beyond the tree, about a quarter of a mile, the Genessee River was flowing through the flat field.

Adams waited a long time for a certain type of cloud and light formation he wanted and finally snapped the picture.

When the brochure was printed, a copy somehow got to the photographic library at the University of Pittsburgh. The head of the library (I think it was a man by the name of Rose), who was a well-known photographer, called me and said, "Jim, you can fool some of the people some of the time," and so forth. I said, "What are you talking about?" And he said, "That isn't a picture of a tree at the end of your brochure, that's a picture of a painting of a tree."

After I explained I had sat there while the picture was being taken, he still wouldn't believe it, and I guess he still doesn't believe it.

The brochure won many awards and is still a collector's item.

There was another star who impressed me when I was a consultant at the University of Rochester. Joe Wilson, the president of the fledgling Xerox Corporation and chairman of the university's board said, "I have a very good friend and lawyer working for us (in fact I've made him chairman of the board of Xerox) and I'd like it if you could use him in some way in connection with the campaign. The fellow's name was Sol Linowitz, a very bright, articulate guy, who later became ambassador to the South American states.

Linowitz came over to our offices and tried to help out, but there wasn't much that I could ask him to do. He was one of the most articulate, brightest guys I've ever met. He also was one of the finest speakers I've ever heard. In any event, I enjoyed knowing him and it probably was my failing that I didn't make more use of him but I think the problem was that there just wasn't any "fit" between what I was doing and what he was able to do.

One of the early recipients of the Michelson Award[2] at Case Institute was Ed Land, the founder of the Polaroid Corporation. Part of my job was to help recipients prepare their remarks which

---

[2] I had long campaigned for a Michelson Award program at Case Institute and I was thwarted by the fact that the idea would take some capital to put it into operation and at the time such an expenditure might have been considered, or was considered, frivolous. The idea was to give an award each year in honor of our famous professor, Albert Michelson, who was a professor of physics at Case just before the turn of the century. I think it is accurate to say that if you ask prominent scientists to name the ten most prominent scientists in the last century, Michelson is always one of them. His research into the "speed of light" was purported to open up the possibility for Einstein's great contributions but I'm not sure that that is accurate. But after pushing for the idea for some time, Kent Smith finally said at a board meeting, "Jim, I know you've wanted to do this for a long time, so I'll put up the money if you want to go ahead and do it." With the help of Bob Shankland, the prominent physicist at Case, we set up a national committee, which each year chose a person who had made the greatest research contribution (much like Michelson) during the previous year. The committee did a magnificent job of choosing the award winners (who received $5,000 and were also asked to make a talk at Case about their contributions). These talk-dinners became, as noted in other parts of this book, tremendously well-attended by 600 to 1,000 of Cleveland's top leaders. Also, of the first seven recipients of the award, it is my recollection that four of them went on to receive the Nobel Prize. Perhaps I am biased, but in my opinion, the award dinner and the publicity surrounding it, was very important in moving Case Institute to the top rung of engineering and science institutions in the nation, as well as internationally.

had to be understandable and interesting to a group of lay people, usually 600 to a 1,000 of Cleveland's finest. We also had a cocktail reception before the actual award dinner which was usually attended by a hundred or so. I remember that Lulu Humphrey told me that they postponed their usual fall trip because they didn't want to miss the Michelson Award Dinner.

Ed Land was one of those unique types who could concentrate to such an extent that when he was concentrating he'd block out the rest of the world. He started to give his speech which was very interesting and included many unusual aspects of light and photography. One picture was a slide of a white cat in a very dark corner of a Spanish courtyard, which had the usual contrasts of bright sunlight and dark shadows. Land said that when he put a light meter up to the cat when they were taking the picture, the meter didn't register any light and yet it was clearly evident that the picture was of a white cat in a dark corner.

In the midst of describing that unusual situation, he noticed something in the picture that he hadn't noticed before. It was immediately evident to me that he had forgotten the hundreds of people who were out there in the audience and was lost in the interesting phenomena which he saw.

I immediately gave him a little tug on his coattail and he came back to the job at hand and completed the talk.

I met Frank Sparks when I participated, at his request, by making a talk at one of the conferences held by the American College Public Relations Association. I then got to know him much better during the time I was a consultant to the Council for Financial Education in New York City where Frank was the president for several years. He was a fine speaker and a very interesting and unique person. Among the things I learned as we traveled together or when he came to visit Cleveland was that he did not attend college at the time most young people do but rather founded Arvin Industries in Indiana. He told me that he set a goal in life of making $300,000 and that he did that so easily through Arvin Industries that he knew there just had to be more to life than $300,000. So he decided to go to college. He was then about 40 years old. He went to Wabash in

Indiana and got his undergraduate degree, a master's degree, and a Ph.D. in three years, which is very, very rare. After getting the Ph.D., they asked him to become president of Wabash College and he agreed. He was very successful in leading Wabash and subsequently was asked to run for governor of Indiana, which he did. Although he was defeated, he told me that he learned one surprising thing. And that was that when you're defeated in a political field, the world doesn't end, but instead many, many other opportunities open up for you. One of those opportunities was the presidency of the Council of Financial Aid to Education. He became one of the most ardent and successful supporters of the Corporate 1% Program.

I met Charles F. "Boss" Kettering when I was a consultant to the Dayton Museum of Natural History when I was with Ketchum, Inc. They asked me to go to Dayton to save the Dayton Museum of Natural History, which was being kicked out of an old factory in which it had been housed for many years. Kettering was interested and I was pleased because I had for a long time been interested in his speeches. Boss Kettering was one of the largest stock holders in General Motors because of his inventions in connection with automobiles. We ultimately saved the museum and got it moved to a new home designed by Richard Neutra, a prominent west coast architect.

As soon as I got to Dayton, they asked me to go out to see Boss Kettering, who had an office in the Winters National Bank in Dayton. When I got there they ushered me into his office which was rather plain. Before I had a chance to ask Kettering many of the questions I had, he, like Fred Crawford, asked me to sit down and began to find out about who I was and what made me tick. He was a lot like Fred Crawford. He was warm and friendly. He told me almost immediately that he was interested in the Dayton Museum and that he had set up trusts for his grandchildren and at various times he would be in position to send along checks which I could use as gifts to the Museum. He said the grandchildren would never miss them. And that is what he did. Of course he was tremendously wealthy and this was before he set up the Kettering Foundation, which is now one of the largest foundations in Ohio. During our conversation, he asked me if I minded if he made an important telephone call. Of course I said, no, and offered to leave, but he asked me to stay. He made the telephone call and it was obvious that it was to someone at General Motors who was in charge of some high level transactions which they were making. I tried not to listen but at the end of the conversation I couldn't help hearing one comment which he made. "Well, I think whatever you do, it should be good for the big stockholder as well as the small stockholder and, as you know, I have a few shares." I was pleased for the opportunity to talk to him and meet him because his speeches that I had read when I was younger were always very interesting. Kettering was not much interested in education. He thought that education stymied a person's ability to think imaginatively. In some of his speeches he would list a number of things like photosynthesis, which, if somebody could figure out how they worked, they would become famous. Obviously he was a creative genius who did not know how good he was.

Victor Babin was dean of the Institute of Music when I was a consultant there. He was not the most important factor in the Institute's fundraising (that crown belonged to Martha Joseph) but Victor was one of the most talented men I have worked with. English was not his first language and he spoke with a fairly strong accent, but he had a depth of understanding of the English language which bordered on "genius." He also was a very talented pianist, a part of the famous piano duo, Babin and Vronsky, who were internationally known. Vronsky was his wife.

We sat together on a flight to New York (we were not on Institute of Music business, but just happened to meet) so we had an opportunity to have a fairly long conversation. One of the things I remember about that flight was that Victor asked me who was my favorite pianist, and I said Arturo Rubinstein, and he said, "Ah, Rubinstein is so good it ought not to be allowed." And then he added, "But Jim, we all must remember that Rubinstein stood on the shoulders of one hundred years of piano excellence spawned by the Warsaw Conservatory."

One time the famous cellist, Gregor Patigorsky, was visiting the Institute and agreed to give an impromptu concert for a small group of prominent friends and students. It was a last minute arrangement and Victor agreed to accompany him. I remember two things about that little concert – one was the unusual perception that Victor, with his unusually strong hands, could have demolished the piano if he wanted to. Another observation was that because it was a last minute arrangement, they both used sheet music and Patigorsky, the cellist, placed his music on a simple music stand. After the first four or five minutes, the music fell off the stand and was strewn all over the floor. Rather than being temperamental and embarrassed about it, both Victor and his friend picked up the strewn music, placed it all back on the stand, and announced that they would start all over again, which they did, and made very beautiful music.

Another time I was talking to Victor and somehow we mentioned Muzak, the music at that time which was piped into a lot of buildings all over the country. Although I thought that Muzak was not the kind of music that Victor would approve of, he surprised me by saying that he thought Muzak was a good thing because it introduced music to many people who would not have the opportunity to listen to music and he thought that any music which might introduce people to music was a good thing.

After returning from Europe at the end of World War II, the dean at the University of Pittsburgh asked me if I could help him by being assistant dean and advise the various returning servicemen who wanted to attend the University under the GI Bill (most were about my age). I planned to go to Harvard Law School, but I told him that if he got in a hole I would try to help him for a short time. Of course, the next day he was "in a hole."

While doing that job at Pitt, the dean said, "Jim, they've called from Carnegie Tech" (which is now Carnegie Mellon) and the dean over there needs an assistant dean and they are willing to pay a very good salary. After a little thought, I agreed to become assistant dean and head of men's dormitories at Carnegie. I decided then to do graduate work at Pitt rather than go to Harvard. I had used up about three-and-a-half years of my life in the Army and the prospect of four years of law school was becoming less attractive.

I spent about a year at Carnegie Tech and then I was accepted for graduate work at Pitt. My graduate work at the University of Pittsburgh included studying with Dr. Percy Hunt, the internationally known expert on Pepys and Shakespeare and an acclaimed teacher of "description and narration." As soon as I started, the director of athletics, Frank Carver, asked me to be director of athletic publicity, which paid a very good salary. When I said, "I'm doing full-time graduate work," he said, "We'll pay you a full salary and you can do your graduate work at the same time, even though you only spend a few hours a day on this job." The job was enjoyable and I developed a very good relationship with the sports writers and was very successful. One of the stories I wrote about a retiring long-time trainer at Pitt made papers all over the country. I said that he was the only man in sports who could get away with "throwing in the towel."

Dr. Hunt suggested that I might get further experience by joining the faculty but I wanted experience outside the university.

I was running the press box at one of the big football games when Carlton Ketchum stopped by and said that my career in the Army, the war, and college administration was the same as his a generation before, and he offered me a job at Ketchum Inc. which was then the number one fundraising firm in the country. I said, "I don't know a darn thing about fundraising," but he just kept upping the salary offer until I said finally, "If you want me that badly I'll come, but what do you want me to do?" He said, "You are a fine writer and you have good experience through your work at Pitt and Carnegie Tech and we want you to lead us into the university and college fund-raising area," which at that time was almost an entirely new field. That started a profitable and fulfilling relationship with Carlton Ketchum and Ketchum Inc. that lasted for nine years.

My first job at Ketchum was at the University of Pittsburgh to publicize the opening of their new field house. Next was a major publicity effort at Pitt that would kick off a major campaign for a new School of Public Health.

I decided to bring the School of Public Health to the attention of the leaders of Pittsburgh via a high level dinner program at the

Mellon Institute, which was housed in a beautiful building adjoining the Pitt campus. We invited about a hundred Pittsburgh leaders, including the Mellons, and the chairmen of Gulf, J & L, and other top corporations.

At that time the University of Pittsburgh medical faculty and medical research area included Jonas Salk, who was working on a vaccine for polio; Cam Moses, who invented the radioactive gold treatment of brain tumors; Thadeous Denowski, who invented the Westinghouse artificial kidney machine; Francis Cheever, an expert on viruses and Dean of the Medical School (his father was Dean of Harvard Medical School) and Dr. Benjamin Spock, the famous "baby book" author.

I got this group together and asked them to help me put on a "Medicine Show." I proposed that each man report on his research for about seven minutes using dramatic backdrops which I would have prepared. Jonas Salk said to me, "Jim, what you want me to do is tell my whole life in seven minutes." Cheever took me aside and said, "If you can get Salk on your side, you can get the others, so I'll give you a little 'course' on viruses to help you to sell Salk." He did, and when we met again, I used 3x5 cards and drew some museum-type backdrop designs including a 15-foot mockup of a beating heart (which would have appropriate sounds). For Salk I prepared a mockup of the polio virus as seen through an electron microscope. Salk asked, "Jim, what do you think I should say?" I said, "Tell them you're working on a polio vaccine and show them the blown-up virus and tell them how you grow it and the various ways you are trying to kill it or partially kill it to produce a vaccine. Tell them that you normally grow it in monkey testicular tissue or by inoculating eggs." I said, "Incidentally, why do you inoculate the eggs?" He burst out laughing and said, "My God, Jim, I thought you knew what you were talking about!" From then on we were all on the same page and the Medicine Show was a huge success as was the effort to fund the new School of Public Health. (Later I worked with Fred Robbins who received the Nobel Prize for discovering how to grow the polio virus.)

I also proved the value of "publicity" in campaigns and the importance of communicating with community leaders.

Next, I went to Carnegie Tech as a consultant to help them prepare a proposal to the Carnegie Foundation, which had many years before offered Carnegie Tech $9 million if Tech would raise an equal amount. Tech didn't think they would be able to raise the money so they didn't try for many years. Now they wanted us to get them started.

Jake Warner, then Carnegie Tech president, a member of the National Academy of Sciences both in chemistry and metallurgy and a great guy, said, "Jim, since you're going to be doing important work, I'd like you to be nearby. We don't have an office nearby so why don't you use the board room as your office and we'll have our meetings when we both go to the john." The board room had what was said to be the biggest table in the world, the "George Westinghouse table." I sat on one end of it and it was like sitting at the end of a bowling alley. But it worked.

Carnegie had an alumni office and a list of their graduates but didn't know their positions and other important information. I devised an alumni survey to get broader information useful in a campaign (titles, company affiliations, etc.). At that time, surveys received about a 1% return. But by asking the right questions and using various techniques including reports of the success of the survey and "timing" of the mailings, I was able to reach a 70% return which was a record and a great step forward, allowing Carnegie to move into the fundraising area. Later, I used these techniques (upgraded) for various clients with even greater success.

Next, I went to the University of Rochester to conduct an effort for $10 million. There I met Joe Wilson who was the founder of Xerox who was chairman of the University of Rochester board. At that time he had a little company called "Haloid" with about $12 million of annual sales. During the time that I was there he said to me, "We have a new development called 'xerography' and if you have $5,000 to invest, I think you should."

Not too many years later I invited him down to speak in Cleveland at the Union Club, and when he got off the plane at Burke

Airport I asked, "Joe, what are all those x's up there?" He laughed and said, "You didn't do it, did you?" And I said, "What would I be worth if I had?" He thought about it and said, "$8 million."

An interesting sidelight on the Xerox story was that Zey Jeffries was a prominent graduate of Case and when I was dealing with Joe Wilson and the Corporate 1% Program and Xerox, Zey Jeffries stopped to see me and during the conversation he said that he was on the board at Battelle Memorial Institute and was the person who talked to Joe Wilson about the xerography research, which was done at Battelle. He noted that Joe Wilson became interested in buying the xerography research and that he was the one who negotiated with Joe about how they would arrange the deal. He said that Joe Wilson wanted to give royalties for the use of the xerography research but that he, Zey Jeffries, held out for stock because he was so sure that ultimately Xerox stock was going to be worth a lot of money. Joe finally agreed and the Xerox stock took off when they began to build the Xerox machines and that stock became, according to Jeffries, a substantial portion of the Battelle endowment.

At this time I was using the various fundraising methods which Ketchum used and they were good in some instances but they were developed mostly for hospital fundraising campaigns and would endeavor to get an entire community involved, including hundreds of solicitors. Great numbers of pledge cards needed to be typed, numerous solicitors trained over long periods of time, with much inefficiency and relatively low returns.

Next, I went to Alliance, Ohio to direct a campaign for Mt. Union College. The accepted method followed by the fundraising firms at that time was to provide the campaign staff "because the clients' employees wouldn't work hard enough." The vice president of Mt. Union, Ron Weber, said, "Since you're going to be running the campaign, I'll have time to run for president of Mt. Union!"

The campaign was successful and he did become president, in due course.

It seemed to me that new methods for fundraising needed to be developed and I had many ideas relative to methods which would be more efficient, less costly, and more successful.

About that time, Ketchum was asked to help with a television effort to promote and ultimately nominate, Dwight Eisenhower for president. It was called "Salute to Eisenhower." Ike was coming back from his great victories in World War II and they were looking for somebody who would be a good MC for the television show, which was the first national TV hook-up of that kind. They couldn't agree on who would be a good MC, and somebody said, "Why not get Fred Crawford?" Somebody else said, "That little fellow in Cleveland? I don't think he's big enough for this job." The remark got back to Fred, I guess, and he decided to "show them." He did, because everyone said he was magnificent, and Eisenhower was nominated.

That was fortunate for me because Fred Crawford was chairman of the board of Case Institute of Technology, a fine engineering and science institution in Cleveland. Case needed someone who could start a development Program. I, and a friend at Ketchum, Harry August, who had been the City Editor of the *Akron Beacon Journal*, decided to investigate. Harry said he would go to Case but only if I would join him because he didn't know much about college fundraising or college administration. I drove to Cleveland with Em and we looked over the city which was very attractive. Even more important was the fact that Cleveland was a diverse community with many top corporations. I then found that 30 Cleveland corporations were on the Fortune 500 List and, in addition, Fred Crawford was chairman of the board of TRW which was one of those major corporations. Also, Cleveland was fairly well known for starting or initiating the first Community Chest, although Rochester, New York, also made the same claim. There was no doubt in my mind that this Community Chest background was a valuable base for anybody who wanted to initiate a development Program at a major Cleveland institution. When I found that the board at Case Institute also was first-rate, I was convinced. Beside Fred Crawford, the board included: Charlie White, chairman of Republic Steel; Hassel Tippit, the managing partner of Ernst and Ernst; Kent Smith, the chairman of Lubrizol; Jack Reavis, the managing partner of Jones Day Coakley and Reavis, one of the largest legal firms in the country; Sid Congden, the chairman of National City Bank; Elmer Lindseth, the chairman of Cleveland Electric Illuminating Company; Bob Ramsdell, the chairman of East Ohio Gas Company; Wallace "Buck" Persons, the chairman of Emerson Electric in St. Louis; George Dively, chairman of Harris Corporation; and John Donnell, vice chairman of Ohio Oil (later Marathon Oil). After talking to the president of Case, T. Keith Glennan, I accepted the job and started in January of 1957.

In addition, I had come to the conclusion that the few colleges and universities which had development offices had only one man heading them and that just wasn't enough to do the job. As part of my acceptance agreement, I got authority to begin to build a staff at Case Institute. Case had conducted a major campaign before I arrived and had promised that it would be their only campaign in that generation. This was a promise that was made several times at a few institutions around the country and with the rapid burgeoning of needs at major institutions, they were promises that could not be kept. So I was faced with overcoming the results of that promise. Fred Crawford was enormously helpful, enabling us to do that.

Shortly after I arrived, the president said that it was very important that we conduct a $6 million campaign and asked me to make a plan so we could get started. I probably wouldn't have taken the job if I had known of one situation which occurred several years before I accepted the job. There was a huge problem which had resulted from a major disagreement between President Glennan and the head of the Case Alumni Association, whose name was "Chappy" Chapman. President Glennan told me the story himself after I was on the job. Apparently when Keith Glennan arrived at Case, Chapman asked for an appointment, and during the appointment said to Keith, "If you keep straight with me, you'll be straight with the Case Alumni." Anybody who knew Keith Glennan knew that this was like trying to stuff a red flag down a raging bull's throat. Shortly after, Chapman tragically died and the chasm which resulted between Glennan and the Case alumni remained for all the years I was connected with Case. My job demanded that I get along with the Case alumni, and I did. Many times when I ran into a problem with the Alumni Association, I said, "Look, have I ever not produced on any promise that I've ever made to you?" And they would answer, "Jim, it's not you -- it's your boss." I should add that this problem was not unusual in the nation at this time. Alumni associations, such as the one at Ohio State and at other institutions, battled with the administrations of those institutions causing untold problems. Pressure to raise millions of dollars to fund the onslaught of the hundreds of thousands of students made it mandatory that the presidents of universities have complete authority over their domains. The result at Case was that in many instances we had to seek the funds needed for Case from foundations, corporations, and other wealthy individuals, and perhaps only ten percent of the very top Case alumni who were not influenced by the "bad blood." However, after I formed my own consulting company, many of the top Case alumni were responsible for hiring me or recommending me to be the consultant to other major institutions in northeastern Ohio.

When Kent Smith became acting president of Case, he called me to say that he had signed a new agreement with the Case Alumni Association and he was sending a copy over to me. I looked at it immediately and called Kent and said, "Kent, do you realize what you've signed?" And he said, "Jim, did I do something wrong?" And I said, "Well, Kent, what you agreed to do was allow the Case Alumni Association to make gifts to institutions other than Case to pay the tuition of sons and daughters of Case alumni." He immediately said, "Get that document back!" Which they did, and he rescinded his agreement. I do not mean to imply that the Case Alumni Association was always wrong and the administration was always right. For example, if you had taken a vote among Case alumni in 1967 on the issue of "the Federation of Case Institute with Case Western Reserve," I'm certain that the Case alumni would have voted against it. It was a very difficult issue and I think even the trustees were split. Looking back from this date (2004) it is very difficult to make a judgment about the success of the "Federation" or merger. My own opinion is that one way of looking at the success of the "Federation" is to compare the stature of the present Engineering

School and the University with two other institutions that I had a long-time connection with -- the University of Pittsburgh where I did my undergraduate and graduate work, and Carnegie Tech (now Carnegie Mellon) where I worked and was a consultant. Those two institutions sit side-by-side much like Case Institute and Western Reserve. My judgment is that both of those institutions have retained national ranking while keeping their own separate identities. However, there is one thing of which I am very certain, and that is that Case Institute of Technology did not receive the amount of financial support after the 1967 Federation that it would have received if it had been a separate institution.

But back to the "campaign" which was not supposed to happen for a generation!

I prepared a long spreadsheet showing how the campaign would develop over a three-year period. I presented the plan to the Case Administrative Council at the president's house on a Sunday afternoon and I took about an hour to explain to the group all the facets of the plan. When I was coming to the end of my explanation, Fred Crawford walked in. He was whistling and had a jolly and positive way of walking very erect. He was rather small, but he looked tall. He came in and sat down beside me and leaned over and said, "Jimmy, what do you have here?" And I said, "Fred, I've got a plan for a capital campaign." And he said, "Oh yeah, uh, huh, uh, huh," running his finger along the major elements of the plan. The president, who had turned away for a moment, turned back and said, "Fred, Jim has a plan for a $6 million campaign and I'd like him to take the time to tell you about it." And I said, "Keith, the 'genius here,' has got it." The president's jaw dropped and I'm certain he didn't believe me, but we talked about that plan for another hour and Fred was "in tune" with the entire "symphony." I knew then that he was a unique, as well as talented, brilliant man. Over the next decades, he proved it scores of times.

It was decided that we should seek approval of the plan from the trustees so we had a board meeting and I presented the plan. When I finished, Charlie White's fist banged the table and he said, "That's the best plan I've ever heard." I think the truth was that

Charlie White just looked at me and thought, "Here's a nice young guy" who needs support. I'm not certain he listened to the plan, but his fist on the table and support were enough to convince everybody else. The board agreed unanimously to go ahead.

One of the important conclusions I had reached about development was that public relations should not be separate from fundraising. The few institutions which had development officers had separate public relations departments. In my opinion, that wasn't the best arrangement. I hired a director of public relations and started to build a development department made up of people who could serve in both PR and fundraising capacities.

At that time the accepted methodology was that corporations, if campaigns were to be successful, should give two-thirds of the goal, although that changed dramatically in a short time. Because of the wonderful Case board I was able to work out a corporation "formula" which spread two-thirds of the $6 million goal according to each corporation's percentage of the total number of employees on the entire major corporation list. Again, a survey became necessary. I conducted a survey to find out where the Case graduates worked and what their positions were, and using the techniques I had developed, we reached a return of more than ninety percent -- a record. This became very important to the success of the campaign. We could give each major corporation a list of Case graduates who worked for them, along with their titles. The campaign was very successful.

Another very important development at that time, which was conceived before I arrived by the president of Case, was the organization of a group called the Case Associates. They were a group of corporations which agreed to give at least $5,000 annually to Case -- quite unusual at that time. The money was used on the operating side of the budget rather than as capital. I took over the Associates program and began to increase the number of corporations who agreed to give at least $5,000 a year (some gave more) and organized them into a group with their own officers that met once a year and were kept up-to-date on Case research and development. The Associates became a tremendous underpinning for the success of the Institute and soon were providing $500,000 annually to our operating budget.

One of the early chairmen of the Case Associates was George Dively, the chairman of Harris Corporation. That started a long-term friendship between George and myself, which ended up with my being a board member on the Dively Foundation. The success of the Associates Program spread very quickly, not only in Cleveland, but nationally and was soon duplicated in many other colleges and universities.

About that time, Frank Joseph, a prominent lawyer who was chairman of the board at John Carroll University, a fine Catholic institution, called me and asked me to be a paid consultant to John Carroll and lead them into the development area. I said, "Frank, I don't think I can do that because I work for Case and I don't know what the trustees would think if you paid me to be a consultant to John Carroll." And he said, "I've already checked your trustees and they agree."

So I became a consultant to John Carroll. Very quickly I came to the conclusion that because John Carroll had an advisory board, a development program would not succeed. You cannot separate authority from responsibility if you are dependent on trustees' leadership. The trustees didn't have authority. Authority resided with a small group of Jesuits who ran the college. I told Father Dunn, the president, who was a fine Jesuit scholar and administrator, that I believed that John Carroll would not compete and might not exist in the not-too-distant future unless it had a board with real authority and responsibility. He sat back and said, "Jim, I don't think there is one chance in fifty that we can do that." But after thinking it over and much discussion, they decided to change from an advisory board to a board that had both authority and responsibility in running the institution. I also pointed out the need for a development vice president. My consulting at John Carroll got a lot of publicity in Cleveland but I soon realized that finding competent development people was one of the major keys to success. For John Carroll, I found a young man, Bill Fissinger, from the University of St. Louis, and recommended him for the position of vice president of development. Over the years I received many plaudits from John Carroll trustees and alumni for the wonderful job I had done, but primarily what I had done was get them Bill Fissinger, and Fissinger was the one who really did the great work!

Shortly after, Frank Joseph's wife, Martha Joseph, called me. She was chairman of the board of the Institute of Music, and she said, "Can you do for us what you did for John Carroll?" And I said, "Martha, I don't want to tell the trustees I want to do more consulting, but I'll try to find you a development person." Subsequently, I found a young man who was getting an MBA at John Carroll and talked to him about taking the job at the Institute of Music. He agreed and was hired. Within three or four months Martha Joseph called me and said, "We're going to have to fire that nice young fellow you sent to us." And I said, "Martha, why would you fire him?" And she said, "Well, he's just not doing the job." And I said, "Martha, don't fire him until I have a chance to talk to him." When I talked to him, he said, "The problem is that when they found out I had an MBA they gave me the extra job of business vice president. I don't have any time for the development area." I called Martha and said, "Martha you are making a big mistake." And she said, "We've already made the decision, Jim, and I don't think I can swing the board of trustees the other way." I replied, "Martha, don't fire him, I'll get him another job and he won't know the difference. He'll go off to the other job and everything will be fine." It worked, and I don't think he knows anything about this, but Jim Mason is now vice president of Eaton Corporation in Cleveland. That gave me another insight into how development consultants should work. I came to the conclusion that if I recommended development officers, I would have to either train them or work with them, and I wasn't ready to do that at that time, so I put the idea in the back of my mind.

About that time I was asked to make a talk at the American Public Relations Association, and one of the things I said was that I didn't think the development area in the country was going to develop the way it should if no one knew the kind of people that should be hired. Most of the few people who were being hired were from sales areas of corporations.

When I finished that speech at the ACPRA, they asked me to head a national study of the qualifications of a development director. I raised some money and hired Hurst Worthington Corporation from Chicago who were psychologically based in the area of executive search. I proposed we get 25 of the best people at universities and colleges in the development area to gather in a central place to do interviews and a study of their qualifications. We got them together in Washington at one of the ACPRA annual meetings and we did the study. (I'm providing a copy of the study to the Western Reserve Historical Society.) The major finding was that successful development officers were not "salesmen." Salesmen have a high degree of "orality" and development people do not. A salesman is selling himself all the time, whether he's in a bar or elsewhere, but a development Officer, while he could perhaps be a good salesman, had to be able to work through other people, such as trustees, and back them with all the necessary proposals, strategy, and information to achieve success. The findings supported the truism I had developed: "People give to people, not to causes." The study was published and spread across the country. It also was put on records and sold. I received many calls and expressions of interest from all over the country from college presidents and others trying to hire development directors. While I never took any money for placing them, I became sort of a Development Placement Center.

I continued to develop a list of new insights and methods in development which were substantially different from those generally accepted. For example, I noticed that successful campaign gift statistics didn't check with what we were saying was true. We said that "ninety percent of the campaign gifts had to come from ten percent of the prospects." I found that much more of the total had to come from far less than ten percent of the prospects. I also found that the idea of corporations giving two-thirds of the campaign goal just wouldn't fly anymore because corporations were being asked to give to many more institutions and causes as the entire area of development progressed.

One of the best campaigns at that time was a campaign for Harvard College. I think it was a successful $30 million effort. When

I looked at the gift statistics, I found that 75% of the $30 million came from the top one hundred prospects, 95% of the total came from the top five hundred prospects including the one hundred, and that all the other hundreds and hundreds of gifts amounted to only five percent. This was a substantial breakthrough in development thinking because it led me to conclude that we were spending much too much time and money on that last five percent (which was really the hardest money to raise). Thus, when I was asked to plan a $16 million campaign for Case I decided to use the percentage method. Actually, this was the first time that this method was used. I proposed that our development committee, over a year's time, solicit the top 100 prospects including corporations, individuals and foundations. I also concluded that the effort needed to be national with individual campaigns in areas where we had sizable alumni concentrations, such as Los Angeles, Chicago, and Boston. This also required a different type of campaign organization and timing. A "Needs" study at this time indicated that Case could use about $62 million of support, and I and the trustees realized we couldn't raise that much.[3]

    I prepared various charts for Elmer Lindseth, then chairman of the board: one each for $6 million, $20 million, and $60 million -- indicating the number and size of gifts needed to achieve these amounts. Elmer then went through the process of negotiating with the president and talking with Kent Smith, who we ascertained would be the first or largest donor. Later, I used this method in almost all my campaigns where I was a consultant and, as mentioned before, this worked out beautifully because it educated the institutions' trustees relative to the gifts needed to achieve success, and their responsibility and the responsibility of the key givers. In the case of this major campaign for Case mandated by the Ford Foundation gift, this method of charting became enormously successful and later was one of the underpinnings of my many consultancies.

---

[3] Almost all "Needs" studies end up higher than the amount of funds that can be raised because of the way they're done: If you ask a faculty department how much they need, the answer usually is astronomical because it's very human to ask for the highest number.

Another important step forward defined the "role" of the president. Most of the presidents were "scholars" but the need for funds was changing their role substantially. For example, the chairman of the board at Temple called me and offered to pay me a "corporate" salary if I became their development vice president. I looked into it and refused. He said, "Would you mind telling me why?" And I said, "Well, confidentially I know that your president has an agreement with his board of trustees that he doesn't have to do any fundraising." And he said, "That's true. Is that the reason why you wouldn't take the job?" I said, "When you ask for a large gift from a foundation, corporation, or individual, they want to talk to the person who's running the place."

This gave me another insight for the future: The head of the institution has to be part of the "team" that does the fundraising. He doesn't have to ask for the gift or make the initial call, but when the person or foundation or corporation says, "Tell me about your institution and what your aims and goals are," the president had to step up and do his bit.

As a result, many colleges and universities which traditionally were run by presidents who were "scholars" began to be run by a combination of a president, a provost who was in charge of the academic program, a financial vice president, and a vice president for development who handled the areas of fundraising and public relations. At Case these areas functioned together as a team. The $16 million campaign came about not only as a result of a study of our needs but also because the provost, who was heading the academic side, developed a $15 million proposal at the request of the Ford Foundation, which wanted to move Case and several other institutions to the forefront of engineering and science education. The Ford Foundation said they would make a gift if we met certain conditions. They agreed to give us $9 million as a down payment if we would raise a total of $16 million including the $9 million.

After we were successful, I figured out how much the $16 million campaign had cost us using some of the new methods I had developed. The cost was approximately $380,000. At that time, the going rate used by major fundraising firms was that the total cost of a campaign would be about fifteen percent of the goal. Also, at that time, Cornell conducted a campaign for approximately $16 million and the cost was reported to be between $2.4 million and $3 million. When we reported these figures to the trustees, Cy Ramo, the "Ramo" in Thomson, Ramo, Woolridge, Inc., who was on the Case board but also was chairman of the board of the California Institute of Technology, said, "I hope you trustees realize that Jim has given us a multi-million gift!" That didn't do my reputation any harm.

Part of our success was due to the fact that the $9 million from the Ford Foundation was a "matching" gift. We had to match some of the $9 million. My plan called for matching it in specific ways, which we did. This led me to understand that "matching gifts" were tremendously important to fundraising in general, and thereafter I stressed the importance of matching. The "matching" idea, I think, had started with the General Electric Company, which initiated a matching philosophy gearing their gifts to increases in annual gifts of university or college alumni to their annual funds.

In the 50's, while I was with Ketchum Incorporated, I was in Stamford, Connecticut, to be part of a group conducting a campaign for the Stamford Hospital. I handled the publicity for that campaign and when it was successful, the story I wrote topped the masthead of the *Stamford Advocate*, which was the major Stamford newspaper owned by Kingsley Gillespie, who told me that the headline was the first to top the masthead at his paper. I mention this because this underscores the importance of publicity for community campaigns, which were conducted in the main for institutions such as hospitals. Also, as a result of that publicity effort, Fred Bowes of Pitney Bowes, offered to nominate me for the Public Relations Society of America (which was a significant honor). I demurred, mainly because I didn't think that my career would go, or should go, in that direction.

I also had a visit from several executives from Yale and Towne, which had sizeable plants in Stamford, even though their headquarters were in New York City, asking me to consider a vice presidency of their company, largely as a result of the pressure that was being brought on them to make a substantial gift to the Stamford

Fifty Golden Years

Hospital campaign (because of the way I handled the campaign publicity). Walter Wheeler, the chairman of Pitney Bowes, which was one of the leading corporations in Stamford, was my willing partner in this "campaign within a campaign."

During my stay in Stamford, a group of Yale University trustees asked me to meet with them so that they could pick my brain. They were an impressive group – all corporate leaders – from the Yale board who lived in the Stamford area. They said that they had recently conducted a very successful campaign for Yale University but in doing so their annual giving had decreased substantially, and they wanted to know why. I questioned the numbers, and they said that the campaign was (I think) for $10 million which was successful, but the consultant to the campaign had insisted they stop their annual fund during the campaign because the consultant thought the duplicate solicitations would cause the campaign to fail (I disagreed with this philosophy which was rampant at that time). I asked them how much they had been receiving in their annual giving when they complied with the consultant's request, and they said that it was around $500,000. I did a quick calculation and said, "I think you lost money." The chairman of the board, who was the head of a legal firm in New York City, thought a moment and then said, "My God, he's right." The point was that if you added up the number of years of lost annual funds and then took the number of years that it would take to bring the annual giving up to the level it was when they stopped it, and put these figures all together, they had lost money!

I had begun to think that another area of development which was being overlooked was "bequests and deferred gifts." Previously I had suggested to the president of Case that we start a "bequest" program to endeavor to get people to put Case in their wills. But he had said, "That won't pay off for ten years or more and both of us will be gone," so we hadn't done it. I persisted and finally it was agreed that we should start a bequest program. I developed a plan and talked to Wallace "Buck" Persons, Case '31, who was chairman of Emerson Electric at St. Louis, and asked him to chair a pilot bequest program for Case. He asked, "What's being done around the country?" And I said, "In general, very few colleges and universities try to get their alumni and friends to put them in their wills, but when they do, they get about one percent of those asked to do so. He asked, "What's the best program that you know of?" I answered, "A University of Pennsylvania program which was conducted recently." "What percentage did they get?" I said, "Ten percent, which was a very fine result." Then he asked, "What are you thinking of as a goal for this pilot program using the Class of '31 at Case?" I said, "One hundred percent!" He smiled and said, "I knew I shouldn't have asked that question." He added, "Jim, my dad brought me by the hand to Case from Painesville and told me that Case was where I was going to go to college even though I was very young at that time."

Years later when Buck decided to enter Case, the dean told him that he had only one chance in fifty of graduating because the Painesville schools didn't have much mathematics at that time and you needed to be well founded in math to succeed at Case. Nonetheless, Buck matriculated at Case, and he not only graduated but became a nationally known high jumper by jumping six foot three inches when the Olympic record was around six feet four inches. He said that when he graduated, the dean handed him his diploma and said, "I did tell you that you had *one* chance in fifty!" But Buck had many other attributes and soon became vice president of Lincoln Electric and then went out to St. Louis to work with Senator Symington at Emerson Electric, and ultimately became chairman.

Case was a very small institution and had only 125 people in the Class of '31, but we set about to bring them together in small groups to ask that they put Case in their wills. At some of the meetings we used Fred Crawford as a speaker and he would make marvelous comments which usually ended with, "The United States is a great country. We're the only country in the world where you can put your assets, represented by some papers, in a safe deposit box and when you take them out years later they'll still be worth something!"

We used the same methods of reporting the successes of the '31 bequest program that I had developed in my surveys mentioned earlier in this book. Without too much effort we were able to get answers from 80 percent of the 125 mostly because of Buck's stature in the class.

Buck also knew he had to be a bequest signer. We held more meetings, and the signers began to grow substantially. When we reached fifty percent, mostly due to Buck's abilities as a salesman, I received a call from Polycarp Kusch, who was a professor at Columbia University and a Nobel Prize winner. He said, "I've received this information from you and Buck and I would like to sign up, but I have eight children and I'm just not able to put Case in my will." I accepted his answer and put it out of my mind. When we reached sixty-five percent, he called again, and in his heavy Austrian accent said, "I capitulate! Stop sending me these reports. I'll sign!" Which he did. We finally reached the total of eighty percent of the 125 graduates of the Class of '31! I estimated that in due course, the pilot operation would produce approximately $35 million for Case. This was a record program in the nation and for Case it became one of the foundations of Case's future development growth.

Each year, the president of Case asked for my predictions for the following year's development receipts, including the amount for bequests, which were usually accurate. He once said to me, "Jim, I don't understand how these estimates you give are so accurate. Can you make people die?" The answer to that question is that when people put an institution in their wills, even though their lawyers tell them not to tell the institution (because if you later take them out of your will "they'll get mad at you"), they're proud and they want you to know. They would call me and tell me about their decision and they would also give their estimate of the ultimate amount. I used those reports to make my estimates. In addition, when someone dies and has an institution in his or her will, a lawyer is usually involved. We would talk to the lawyer and he would often indicate that even though it might take a year or two before the will would be finally settled, he could make an "unofficial" estimate of the amount. The bequest area soon became an important area of development at Case and in the nation.

During this time, I was elected president of the board of Education of the Orange School System. Ralph Besse, chairman of CEI, and Art Holden, chairman of the Martha Holden Jennings Foundation, asked me to become chairman of a major research project to judge the effectiveness of school systems across the country. It was an area which was interesting to me, and I realized the key to judging the effectiveness of school systems was to separate the home, where a lot of education takes place, from the school, and find a way to measure which systems were doing the best job and how they were doing it. The Jennings Foundation was dedicated to education below the college and university level and Art Holden said that the foundation would provide all the money I needed to do this job. I proposed that I form a board and that Ralph Besse become the first member of that board. He agreed. I then asked Kelvin Smith, who was then chairman of Lubrizol and whose father had been a great teacher of physics at Case, to come on the board, and he agreed. I also talked to David Morgenthaler, one of the country's leading venture capitalists whom I had known in Pittsburgh many years before and he agreed to join the board. Herold Hunt, Elliot Professor of Education at Harvard and former superintendent of the Chicago school system, also agreed.

At that time, we had three professors at Case who were doing interesting work in what is now known as systems analysis but at that time was called "operations research." They had written a book on operations research which was published by John Wiley & Sons. My office received the royalties from some textbooks written by Case professors, and I noticed that this book was spreading all over the world -- Germany, Japan, France, England, etc. I knew that these fellows were on to something. I talked with them and asked them if they could help me with the research in the area school systems, and they agreed. In the interim, one of them, Russ Aycoff, became head of operations research at the University of Pennsylvania's Wharton School, and Churchman, who was another of the three, agreed to be a professor of operations research at the University of California. The third, Leonard Arnoff, stayed at Case for a while and then moved to become head of operations research at Ernst & Ernst. Ernst & Ernst (and Arnoff) agreed to help in this research for a fee. Ralph Besse then proposed that I receive a fee for my work as chairman of

Fifty Golden Years

the board of the project. Subsequently, we published a monologue which went to every library in the country. I was co-author, along with my friend, Professor Bob Shurter, who was a noted teacher and developer of the Western Civilization Course at Case. We called the program, "The Yardstick Project."[4]

When St. Luke's Hospital, which at that time was chaired by Charlie Arter, asked me to be a consultant, I decided it was time to put the ideas I had in operation and become a full-time consultant. I left Case on June 30th of 1969, and opened three offices -- one next to the Cleveland Foundation in the National City Bank Building, one in the Alcazar Hotel in University Circle, and one in my home, to handle these various projects. We hired a president for the Yardstick Project, Fred Pinkham, who had been president of Ripon College, and Keith Shook of Alcoa, to be president of the Corporate 1% Program.

I also was asked by the Vocational Guidance and Rehabilitation Center Services (VGS) to help steer them into the development business. VGS gives an annual award to its most successful "client" (by the term "clients" VGS refers to the people included in the VGS training programs). It's interesting to note that the award is in honor of Fred Crawford, and it is called "The Fred Crawford Award." This was important to me because VGS was a long-time service agency which received almost all its support from government and other public funds except for three trustees who "covered" an occasional deficit. These trustees (David Swetland, chairman of the Sears-Swetland Foundation, Bob Gries, chairman of the Gries Foundation, and Jock Collins, who had been a vice president of Reliance Electric) said that VGS was not going to be able to count on government support for long and needed to get into the development area if it was going to continue to be successful. VGS had no "constituency," no alumni group or list of supporters, so we

---

[4] "Yardstick" is separate from the area of philanthropy, which is the principal subject of this book, but I've included it because fees being paid to me were growing and the possibility of becoming a full-time development consultant was becoming a reality.

had to start from scratch. I proposed that I find them a development officer, and that I become a consultant and train the development officer and put them in the development business. I worked out a contract which became the prototype of all contracts that I used with clients. It called for a certain amount of time, usually one day a month, in "active" consulting, one day a month in preparation and follow-up, and one day for phone contact with four or five specified people representing the client.

To begin the VGS consultancy I decided that since the "top 100" people in a campaign give seventy-five percent of the total, why not turn that idea around and try to get 100 "leading" people interested in building a development program at VGS? VGS did have a historic tie to a group of women who many years before had decided to spend some of their time helping the handicapped. Most of them were daughters of wealthy Clevelanders. They met periodically and sewed clothing for the handicapped. We had a record of those young people and knew which ones were still living. We decided that we would ask them to attend a meeting along with other community leaders and tell them why it was necessary for VGS to get into the development business. I said if we could get 100 interested prominent people ultimately to come to such meetings and show interest we would be able to start to build a successful development program.

We were successful in achieving that goal. The two people who were most responsible in making that process work were VGS trustees Mrs. Eleanor Zeising and "Chappie" McBride. That led me to believe, as I still do, that women can be very successful volunteer leaders in the development area even though they are not chairmen or presidents of major corporations.

I then decided to implement the large meetings with "Special Luncheons" to which we invited just two to five compatible community leaders and gave them an opportunity to talk with us and ask some questions. The key to the success of the luncheons was their "quality" and the fact that we conducted them in a very short time. We told the "invitees" that if they came promptly at 12:00, we would have them out and on their way at 1:30. We also kept the program to a minimum. It usually consisted of about seven minutes in which the president or chief executive spoke about the institution and its goals and the remainder of the time was used for questions and answers. These special lunches were usually chaired by a trustee who invited three to five community leaders he or she knew personally. This was usually doable if the trustees were flexible enough in setting the date. Also, taking a page from college "annual funds", I proposed that we develop a VGS "annual fund" and ask people to make annual gifts which would support the operations of the institution. We built the list very carefully.

In developing these Special Luncheons for various clients, we were very careful in the way they were set up. First we tried to find a very attractive place in the institution, usually a small dining room or an area in a library for the luncheon. We often had a very special table built for the luncheons because I believed it was very important that only one conversation at a time be held at the special luncheon table. The table usually was either round or octagonal and seated just eight people so that when a conversation took place, or a question was answered, everybody was part of the discussion. At Case we built a special room which we called the President's Dining Room above the gym with large windows that overlooked the gym so that the guests could see the fine young Case people who were usually practicing or playing basketball down in the gym. At St. Luke's, the carpenters built a special table. We made certain that the food that was served was the kind of food a major community leader would expect. In one instance at the Institute of Music, the chairman of the board, Martha Joseph, made a very special casserole, which added to the success of the luncheon. The importance of the timeliness of the luncheons should not be underestimated. I remember a phone call from Frank Milbourne, the chairman of Coe Manufacturing Company in Painesville, who said, "Jim, I want to thank you for the meetings that you run." And I said, "Frank, I don't know that we had a meeting recently which you attended." And he said, "I know that, but I went to a meeting at another institution and it lasted so long that I decided to call you and thank you for the meetings you run."

One of the early innovations I developed was to have key people on the board of trustees attend a very special meeting where we displayed personally addressed and typed letters to those who were on the annual fund list. We asked the trustees to add little notes to the letters such as "Dear X, I'm a trustee at this institution and I hope you will consider making an annual gift." Later, this technique was used by almost all institutions, but many of them didn't understand that the notes had to be "personal" and written by someone close to the person being asked. This technique really was part of the "people give to people" truism which I mentioned earlier in this overview.

One of the early examples of this special technique that I remember was a note that Darwin Noll, chairman of Cardinal Corporation, wrote on a special letter to Sam Miller, a major Cleveland leader and a friend of Darwin's. Darwin wrote, "Dear Sam, I see that you just received $8,000 for being a referee in a legal contest. Just send along the $8,000 and I'll be happy." A few days later, VGS received a note to Darwin from Sam Miller, "Someone else beat you to it, so all I can give you is half of the $8,000."

It was becoming evident that the major elements of institutional development should include annual funds (for operations support), endowment funds (usually from wills), and capital funding (for buildings), public relations, and periodic campaigns, usually to fund building and endowment needs.

Proposal writing covering major requests to foundations, corporations, and philanthropic individuals became increasingly important.

Also, record keeping, public relations, and publications grew in importance.

The accepted method in major campaigns at this time was to have what was called a "major brochure" outlining the objectives of the campaign and how it was going to be conducted. It was usually a very costly publication, beautifully done. I can remember several that cost $25 or $30 a copy which was a substantial amount of money at that time. I had written and produced many brochures in my time with Ketchum, Inc., some of which won national awards. One that

I wrote and designed and got ready to be published in one week of consulting for the Ball Memorial Hospital in Muncie, Indiana, won the national award as the best brochure that year for a small hospital. However, I came to think that major brochures were unnecessary as my consulting evolved. Many times, by the time the brochure was written and produced, all of the various objectives had changed, so it was a waste of money.

I was asked to become a consultant to the Cleveland Playhouse after they had hired several consultants who had spent a lot of time and money developing a major brochure. The consultants subsequently "struck out" and I said, "If I become a consultant I want you to know that those brochures sitting in that back room are going to be useless." And they said, "We know that -- they're already useless." So I began to think that major brochures were not necessary. Also, printed pledge cards were usually used for major donors early in campaigns, and I felt that wasn't the way to do it because major donors were very special and printed pledge cards didn't indicate that anybody was very special. So I decided that when soliciting the top "100 gifts," we would just do away with the pledge card; we used them later in the campaigns.

However, I did find that a "memorial" brochure, a nicely done brochure covering the "memorials" available in a capital campaign was an important technique. We asked the architect to draw actual floor plans showing the outline of the various rooms or areas to be built and then designated them as potential memorials or tributes that people could "buy" in memory or as a tribute to a loved one or some other person. The technique of pricing these various rooms or facilities became of key importance.

There were many elements which went into the value of a memorial. For example, a hospital lobby, which might not cost nearly as much as a major kitchen to construct, was valued at many times that of the kitchen because everybody who came into the hospital or that building had to pass through the lobby, but few ever saw the kitchen. If this technique was done right, often every major or even minor memorial was "sold" as a part of a capital campaign.

In addition, I decided that "feasibility" studies, which were done by major fundraising firms at that time, were useless because of the way they were done. Usually someone from the fundraising firm would ask the top trustees of the institution to write letters to fifty major leaders in the town saying that they were planning a campaign and would like "x" to talk to you and get your opinion. "X" was usually a young man who would say when he met with each of the fifty, "This is what we plan to do, are you in favor of it?" And almost always, the answer was, "I really don't know much about it, but sure, I'm for progress." And then the interviewer would say, "If we conduct this campaign, would you give?" And the answer usually was, "I don't know that I would but I'd certainly think about it." And then the next question was, "Would you give substantially?" And usually the fellow would smile and say, "Well, what's substantial for one person isn't substantial for another." And then he would often add, "But I don't want to be chairman!" The interviewer would then go back to the office and get out a boiler plate document that would recommend that the institution could campaign for $1 million, $2 million, or $3 million, etc. I knew that this was useless. When I started consulting I said that these were useless, and many of the people who talked to me said they had come to the same conclusion. Some had done three or four costly feasibility studies, none which had led to anything important for the institution.

For example, I was asked to meet with two people, one of them was Darwin Noll, and the other a potential major donor, Jerry O'Neill, who headed a major foundation, asking me to become a consultant to St. Vincent Hospital, a fine Catholic hospital in downtown Cleveland. They said St. Vincent needed $15 million to start a research project in the area of the heart. The major researcher was to be their famous heart doctor, Dr. "Bud" Kay, the co-developer of the "Cross-Kay Oxygenator." They said they needed $15 million, but a feasibility study by a major fundraising company indicated they could raise only $8 million. I said, "I can't tell you right now how much money you can raise but I can tell you that I can think of three foundations that are interested in St. Vincent's Hospital who must give substantially in any successful campaign for St. Vincent's.

If they could be asked for $3 million each which would amount to $9 million, I think that you might get the "top 100" to give 75 percent of the $15 million. They said getting that much from those three entities (one of them was the major foundation represented by Jerry O'Neill) was close to impossible. I said, "Why not give it a try and if you ask them and they agree, I'd be glad to do the consulting, and if they don't, you'll be free to find somebody else to do the consulting and you will not have spent any money?" In due course they talked it over and came to a conclusion that it was possible. The three ultimately pledged $9 million even though the feasibility study had concluded they could raise only $8 million from an entire campaign!

In addition, I knew that much costly time was wasted in major campaigns by asking person after person to be the campaign chairman, and failing to find anybody who would do it. I knew that there usually were about seven or eight prominent people (usually trustees) in any institution who really had a vital interest in the project. I would propose that they become a campaign steering committee and ask them to meet one day a month for lunch (one-and-a-half hours) for twelve months to evaluate and solicit the "top 100" prospects who would provide seventy-five percent of the total. I knew that almost no interested trustee would turn down a request to attend one luncheon meeting a month lasting no more than one hour and a half.

They would say, "Who's going to be chairman of the committee?" And I would say, "Let's not worry about that, let's have the chairman of the trustees or someone else serve as the "convener" of the committee, and the campaign chairman will become evident as we go along." And that's the way it worked out. Usually when somebody saw that this really wasn't that difficult and wasn't time consuming, they just sort of evolved into the job.

We first asked the committee to "evaluate" the first 25 or 50 of the "top 100" and that became a very important part of the effort. "Evaluation," or the estimates of amounts that the prospects we were discussing **could** give (not what they **would** give, but what they could give usually over a period of three years, if they were interested) was the key to the campaign. The discussion of the prospects usually produced someone on the committee who said, "I know him and I know he could give $100,000 over a three-year period if he's interested." That led us to the person who was going to do the asking, usually the same person who said, "I know him well," so that the numbers derived from these discussions comprised a far better feasibility study than the studies that were being conducted up to that time (without the necessary input of the major trustees interested in the institution). I knew that the amounts that might be asked from the most important prospects, perhaps only 25, would begin to educate the committee on whether or not the campaign amount was feasible. In fact I soon was able to come up with charts showing the amounts and the number of gifts needed for success. I developed a mathematical model relating various goals to the top 10, top 5, and "top 100." For example, I would make a chart saying we need "two gifts of $500,000," "five gifts of $100,000," "ten gifts of $50,000," etc., so that in our discussions we were zeroing in on the actual gifts needed over a three-year period. One time, Claude Blair, the chairman of the National City Bank, said to me, "Jim, I've watched you make these charts for many years and have seen how accurate they proved to be at the end of the campaign and I still don't know how you do it." I admit there's a little bit of psychology in it but it needs to be also backed up by experience and an understanding of the people who are doing the asking and the people who are being asked to give. Thus, one of the most important things that makes for the success of a campaign is the makeup of the campaign steering committee. I would add that the one thing a consultant can't teach a development officer is the ability to influence the makeup of that campaign steering committee. I think the best development consultants have unusual abilities to judge the makeup of those committees and to influence those committees. It is also important that the campaign consultant understand the basic generosity of the American people. He or she must understand that people will give if they're asked to give by the right person. I remember once a major Clevelander said to me, "I don't know who could ask me to do what you say should be done." And I said, "Fred Crawford."

And he smiled and said, "You named the one person who could do it. I couldn't turn him down." That is what gave people like Fred Crawford the tremendous influence that they had. So many people respected him, wanted to be with him, and thus if he asked them, tried to do what he asked.

Another important technique in the success of a development program which I have not yet mentioned is that each institution should have a top flight development committee. A development committee is much like, and functions like, the campaign steering committee and should be made up of the finest, strongest people, usually trustees, that the institution has. Often times, the executive committee of the board of trustees is a carbon copy of the development committee or vice versa. I've often said that if I could choose the people who should be on the development committee and if they would serve, I would agree to raise almost any reasonable amount of money needed. Generally these people are those who have made many gifts throughout their lives and when they decide to serve on a committee which does the major asking, they are actually taking from a huge pot that they have filled during their entire lives.

One of the best examples of that procedure was when I became a consultant to Western Reserve Academy, a fine private institution in Hudson, Ohio. John Ong, who was then chairman of Goodrich Corporation, was chairman of the board of the academy, and chaired the meetings of the steering committee, which included Jim Knight, who was one of the two brothers who had founded Knight-Ridder Corporation. Jim, a very wealthy man, had been kicked out of Western Reserve Academy years before. When I suggested that we might ask Jim Knight to serve on the committee, John Ong said, "He lives in Miami and you can't expect him to come up to Hudson, Ohio, to attend a one and one half hour meeting once a month." I said, "I know he likes to play golf and has his own plane, so why don't you ask him to fly up to Hudson and we'll have the meeting and then he can play golf. He might like to do that." George McCuskey, who was head of Arthur McKee Manufacturing Company on the west side of Cleveland, was on the committee and was an avid golfer, and he said, "I'd be glad to play with him if he'd come up." John Ong called Jim Knight and he agreed to join the committee, and he attended every meeting. As agreed, there were twelve meetings during that first year, and the only one he didn't fly up for was the final one. For the final one, he said, "I've flown up here for every meeting so far, so why don't we have the final meeting in Miami and all you guys can come down to my place." That's the way it worked out. Ultimately, Jim Knight also gave $1 million dollars, and the campaign was very successful.

Earlier, when we had discussed the first 25 or 50 of the "top 100" and "evaluated" them, John Ong said, "Jim, at the next meeting let us know your idea of how much we can raise." They needed $6 million and I said to him, "John, you're a bright guy and you've been through this process. I've explained how it works and I'll come up with the number, but you put a number down that you think we can raise and have it in your pocket. When I give you my number at the next meeting, pull it out and let's see how close we are." At the meeting I said I thought we could raise $4 million (remember that they needed $6 million) and John Ong pulled out his piece of paper and he had the same number, $4 million. He said, "Jim, what are we going to do?" And I said, "We need two gifts of $1 million each in addition to what we've evaluated or maybe one or two of the people we discussed and evaluated at lesser amounts could give a million." He thought about it and we met a few days later and he said, "I've come up with two entities that I think could give a million each." And I said, "Let's solicit them first. If they don't agree, we haven't expended any great amount of money and we can lower the goal." He agreed and we subsequently got a million from each of the prospects and began the campaign for $6 million. It was very successful.

The validity of the importance of a development director or a development vice president was shown again when I was asked to be a consultant at Hathaway Brown, a fine Cleveland private girls school.

When they hired me and asked me to get them into a major campaign, I noted that they would need a development officer and I said that among all their women graduates, there must be a number of them who could qualify as a development director. At that time,

I think that there was no private school in Cleveland that had a development director.

They asked me to suggest someone who might do the job and I agreed to look over their alumni and perhaps suggest three who might qualify.

I researched the material they provided for me and I came up with three excellent candidates. I fully expected the Hathaway Brown administration to make the choice but they didn't seem to think that anyone would accept the job or maybe it was just that they got "cold feet." In any event, they asked me if I would do the interviews and make the choice. I reluctantly agreed to do so. I proceeded to interview the three candidates. One of them was Edna Strnad, who had been, I think, a copy editor for a New York magazine, and was married to Bud Strnad, president of the LEMCO company in Cleveland, and undoubtedly had a great deal of affection for Hathaway Brown. She also had substantial stature among the Hathaway Brown alumni and ultimately became one of the best development directors I worked with because of her excellent judgment, intelligence, and dedication.

We agreed that her salary would be $12,000 a year and that she would have substantial latitude in choosing the hours she would work. (Of course the way it worked out, because of the type of person she is, she ended up working harder than most people work full-time.)

In addition, it's my recollection that when Edna retired, she gave her entire salary back to Hathaway Brown as a gift.

For many years, her husband, Bud Strnad, kidded (I think) that I had really cost him a great deal of money. He said Edna's salary cost him from an income tax standpoint; it also cost him because Edna was often busy when he wanted to do something else; and Edna's involvement required him to give much more than he might have otherwise done, to Hathaway Brown.

The entire process, however, proved to many Clevelanders that there were women in Cleveland who had substantial abilities and that women could become excellent development directors.

Since then, legions of women have entered the development field even though at that time, Edna certainly was one of the first.

Looking back over the fifty years of philanthropy, one of the most important contributions I made was to influence and train new development officers or vice presidents. At one time, I looked over the roster of people who were serving as development officers in Cleveland and northeastern Ohio institutions, and I counted 22 that I had trained or recommended for the position, or influenced in some major way.

I always thought of it as "training myself out of a job." In other words, I would recommend the development officer, work with him or her in a major campaign or to start a development program, and move to a point where I could leave and the new development officer could carry on alone.

But many times, or at least some times, it didn't work out that way.

For example, I was a consultant at St. Luke's for more than 20 years, which also included two major campaigns. I was also a consultant at Vocational Guidance for 20 years and worked with at least five development officers at that time. However, "VGS" as we called it, chose their own development officers and asked me to train them and work with them. It helped that Ted Fabyan, the VGS executive, at one time in his career was a development officer himself, and the development officers he hired over those years (there were at least six of them) were for the most part, excellent candidates.

Many of the people I worked with became life-long acquaintances including Eldon Winkler (vice president of Lake Erie College, then director of development at St. Luke's and then almost to the end of his life, a director of development at Salvation Army in Florida); "Bunny" Loomis, director of development at Beechbrook; Bill Bowen, director of development of the Museum of Natural History, then a top administrator at the Salvation Army and then executive director of the Case Alumni Association; Jim Joseph (one of my top staff members at Case), then director of a major educational research project, then various top positions at hospitals and corporations, then important jobs in southern Ohio and an award-winning professor; August Napoli, director of development at Ursuline College, top development officer in the Cleveland Catholic Diocese, president of Catholic Charities and now, vice chairman of The Cleveland Clinic Foundation; Jim Szubski, director of development, Museum of Natural History, then the development director of Akron Art Museum; Lynn Feighan, director of development at Laurel School, then director of development at the Cleveland Garden Center -- later changed to Cleveland Botanical Center; Brian Cantlin, director of development at the Ohio College of Podiatric Medicine, then director of development at St. Luke's Hospital and later development officer at the Case Alumni Association; Sue Martens, secretary (Glen Oaks School), development officer, Breckenridge Presbyterian Retirement Center, Cleveland Museum of Natural History, then the Cleveland Clinic; Pat Scalzi, Western Reserve Academy, then CWRU, and finally Arizona State University; Bob Toth, St. Vincent's Hospital, then Visiting Nurse Association; Joe Mills, development director of CWRU, Lake Erie College, Rainbow Babies and Children's Hospital, then vice president of a college in Texas; Stan Trupo, development officer, Cleveland Museum of Natural History, then Lorain Community College, and finally Mayor of Berea; Tara Busser Blazer, development specialist, Museum of Natural History, now executive director, Rockford Art Museum.

Fred Crawford used to call me and say (when one of the institutions we were interested in needed a development officer), "Jim, get one of those good young people who don't know how good they are."

As noted elsewhere, corporate giving does not amount to the largest percentage of the total giving in any year, but has a far greater importance in total philanthropy than the statistics show. Much of the leadership in philanthropic efforts is provided by corporate leaders. I believe that corporate leadership in Cleveland (from TRW, Republic Steel, Eaton, Lubrizol, etc.) is one of the major reasons for the success of philanthropy in the 50 Golden Years. For example, during the 50 years, National City Bank provided leadership to many of the efforts in Cleveland. When I joined Case, Sid Congden was chairman of National City, and was prominent on the Case board. Later, Claude Blair became chairman of National City and took leadership in many philanthropic efforts. Ed Brandon became chairman later and provided leadership in many efforts, including a very successful effort for Notre Dame College (the one in Ohio). For a short time, John Fangboner came to Cleveland to be chairman of National City and it's interesting to note that he came to see me at Case and said that he was from the East and he needed to quickly get to know as many prominent people in Cleveland as he could. He said that everybody told him that if he wanted to do that he ought to go to work for Case. And so he presented himself as being available to go to work for Case. Lubrizol had a substantial effect on philanthropy in the 50 years, not only through their corporate giving, but by passing down leadership roles to their various officers including Alex Nason, Kelvin Smith, Kent Smith, Tom Mastin, and Roger Clapp. For example, Tom Mastin, when he was chairman of Lubrizol, besides his interest in Grand River Academy, contacted me about his interest in the Museum of Natural History (he was an expert on bees and their various ways of communicating) and he told me that although he had negative feelings about the then director of the museum, Hal Mahan, he wanted to make a $600,000 "life income" gift to the museum. A life income gift pays the donor a certain percentage of interest for a number of years, sometimes until the donor dies, and then reverts to the recipient institution. I'm not certain, but I think Tom subsequently turned the contract over to the museum.

  Corporate leadership in the 50 Golden Years was centered in a very few corporations. When I came to Cleveland in the 50's, there were 30 Cleveland corporations listed in the Fortune 500 list of major corporations (now there are only about ten). I think 30 was the largest number in any city except for New York and Chicago. The leadership corporations in Cleveland were Republic Steel Corporation, headed by Charlie White; TRW, headed by Fred Crawford; the Standard Oil Company of Ohio, headed by Charlie Spahr; Harris Corporation headed by George Dively; Lubrizol Corporation headed by Kent Smith; the Warner and Swasey Company, headed by Walter Bailey and later Jim Hodge; the Stouffer Corporation, headed by Vernon Stouffer; the Midland-Ross Corporation, headed by Wade Harris; the Pickands Mather and Company, headed by John Sherwin; the Cleveland Twist Drill Company, headed by Arthur S. Armstrong; the Tremco Manufacturing Company, headed by Bill Treuhaft; the Weatherhead Company, headed by Albert Weatherhead, Jr.; and East Ohio Gas, headed by Bob Ramsdell. It is very interesting to note that most of these leadership companies took leadership in the Corporate 1% Program for Higher Education and were charter signers.

One of the most important facts to know about philanthropy is that although (during the 50 golden years) total giving in the United States grew annually, and was somewhere in between $50 billion and $150 billion, most of the money was given by individuals. In my talks to groups, including the most influential people in our community, I would ask the question, "Of the $150 billion given by Americans, which groups give the most?" The answer usually was, "Foundations." When I said, "Foundations only give perhaps $6 to $10 billion, who do you think gives the rest? The answer usually was "Corporations." And when I said, "Corporations give only about as much as the foundations," the group was usually astonished. Then I would tell them that ninety percent of the total giving comes from individuals "like you and me."

During the 50 Golden Years, no other country had this remarkable record of giving. At the end of the 50 years, Japan and Great Britain started to get some success in philanthropy, but I'm convinced that the rich tradition of giving in the United States is one of the reasons for the remarkable success of our democracy. And it's important to note that while the number of individual givers is relatively small in a capital campaign or in support of a major institution, their leadership is tremendously important in getting other people to follow their leadership. That is why "leadership gifts" in any major philanthropic effort are so important.

One of the reasons that individuals are so important in the overall giving total is because of "personal solicitation" which I have mentioned many times in this book. As I have said before, "People give to people, not to causes." If someone, who is the right person does the "asking" (one of the important tasks in a capital campaign is to find that right person) success usually follows. And equally important is that you must "ask." Often times after a successful effort, leaders of the campaigning institution have come to me and said, "Jim, one of the most important things you've taught us is that we must "ask." A good example of this occurred in a $6 million campaign for the Cleveland YMCA for which I was the consultant. In doing some research into the fundraising background of the Cleveland YMCA, I noted that they had conducted a small effort in the past and that Theo Moll had been one of the leaders of the West Side effort of that campaign. I knew Theo Moll very well and I knew that he was one of the most generous philanthropists in the Cleveland area. He was a major donor to Fairview General Hospital, the Cleveland City Mission, the Salvation Army, and the Elyria Methodist Home. However, I noted that in the period after the time when he was one of the leaders of that West Side effort for the YMCA, that he made no other gifts. I asked the leadership of the YMCA why there were no further gifts from Theo Moll and the best that I could ascertain was that he hadn't been asked, even though the YMCA had an annual fund. I soon came to the conclusion that what had happened was that they had in their earlier annual fund drive, asked for gifts of $100 a year from a reasonable number of people and they just kept going back each year and getting the same $100 even though there had been substantial inflation and substantial increased needs. When I started the "Top 100" gift solicitation for the $6 million campaign, solicitors got a personal interview with Theo and his opening statement was, "Where have you fellows been all this time?" He then proceeded to make one of the largest gifts to that campaign, which was very successful. Another major giver to that campaign was Dick Jacobs who later became the owner of the Cleveland Indians and who was not known as a major philanthropist in Cleveland. But after a well-planned personal solicitation for the YMCA, he made one of the largest gifts to that campaign.

Almost every institution has some individuals who are interested in them and an effort to organize a group to personally solicit them individually is always one of the pillars of success.

Otto Donnell was the founder of Ohio Oil and although he died before I joined Case Institute of Technology, he was responsible for a sizeable "mystery" gift to Case after I became vice president. One day I received a notification that we had received $300,000 from John Teagle, who had been chairman of Standard Oil of New Jersey. I couldn't find any tie between Case and Standard Oil of New Jersey or Teagle, and I began research to find out why we had received the gift. The answer, I finally found, was that Mr. Teagle sat next to Otto Donnell at the speaker's table at a prominent meeting. During the meeting he mentioned to Otto Donnell that he was completing his will and he couldn't find enough institutions to give his money to. And Otto Donnell said to him, "Well, I'm a graduate of a little institution in Cleveland, Ohio, Case Institute of Technology, and if you're looking you might add them to your list." And that's exactly what Teagle did. So Case got a major gift at that time as a result of a "chance" conversation.

It is interesting to note that because of wealth, family foundations, and most of all, philanthropic tradition, many sons in Cleveland have followed their fathers in philanthropy. Some that come to mind are David Ingalls, Sr. and David Ingalls, Jr., Maynard (Bud) Murch and his father, Boynton Murch, John Sherwin and his father, John Sherwin, Sr., John Donnell and his father Otto Donnell, Carlisle Tippit and his father, Hassel Tippit, Jon Lindseth and his father, Elmer Lindseth, "Linc" Reavis and his father, Jack Reavis. I shouldn't forget the female side of the ledger which would include Lulu Humphrey and her father, R. Livingston Ireland, and her son, George Humphrey, Cara Stirn and Lucia-Nash and their parents, Kelvin and Eleanor Smith, Ruth Eppig and her father, David Swetland.

No one could be connected with philanthropy for more than 50 years without learning a bit about foundations. When I was doing some work in Pittsburgh years ago, there was a foundation which was set up on the north side of Pittsburgh to provide coal to the people living along a certain street. It grew until there was a substantial amount of money in the foundation, but no one left to give coal to.

It is very difficult to change the purposes of a foundation, but a smart group of people went at it and finally were able to change the charter of the foundation so that the money could be given for some other useful purposes. However, there are many instances where a foundation is founded with very specific purposes and the original founder dies and either his lawyer or another member of the family takes over. Thus, the actual purposes can change a hundred and eighty degrees or even three hundred and sixty degrees. A famous case is the Ford Foundation where Henry Ford's son actually resigned from the foundation board because the board was using the money for purposes completely opposite from what Henry Ford would have wanted. There are instances such as this in Cleveland and one that I can think of is the Prentiss Foundation set up by Elizabeth Severance Prentiss' sizeable estate. She had one of the most famous and excellent lawyers in Cleveland, Robert Bingham, Sr., draw up an excellent charter following her directions. She wanted the money to be used to found St. Luke's Hospital. Her "new" husband had been chief of staff at University Hospitals and the medical staff kicked him out while they were on their honeymoon in Europe, so she founded St. Luke's so that he would have a hospital to serve as chief of staff. She asked that the foundation be drawn up primarily for St. Luke's, so the charter called for St. Luke's to have first-call on foundation grants and also get half of the income from the foundation each year. If the managers, as they were called, didn't approve grants to St. Luke's, the charter stipulated that St. Luke's could call together a special community group to look at the proposal and have another shot at getting approval. Over the years, St. Luke's received a large amount of the money from the foundation, mostly through the stipulation giving half the income to St. Luke's. But as time passed, other members of the Prentiss relationship were put on the board of managers and a great deal of the grant money started to go to University Hospitals, the very place to which Mrs. Prentiss was opposed.

When I became a consultant to St. Luke's and we started a development office and launched a $17,250,000 campaign, chairman Charlie Arter, John Hadden (who was a manager of the foundation), and I decided to try to get a major gift in addition to the income from the foundation for St. Lukes. At that time, Severence Milliken, a relative of Mrs. Prentiss, was the lead manager and nobody would challenge him when he decided each year to give more and more money to University Hospitals. We prepared a very logical proposal for $1 million and presented it to the foundation. John Hadden, one of the founders of the law firm, Arter and Hadden, went to Severence Milliken, who was a very powerful man in Cleveland, and said, "Severence, I've gone along with everything that you have proposed over the years and we've always had a unanimous vote, but this time I'm not going to do that. I think St. Luke's deserves the million dollars and I'm going to vote against you. A University Hospital man to the end, Severence Milliken said, "Okay, I'll approve the $1 million for St. Luke's but I think we should also give $1 million to University Hospitals."

Another time when I was a consultant to the Health Museum, Kelvin Smith proposed that we make a proposal to the Prentiss Foundation for a grant to the Health Museum because the museum was started in the original Prentiss house on Euclid Avenue. Kelvin said he would try to get some of the members of the Prentiss family together to see what could be done. The Smiths were related to the Prentiss family through Mrs. Nash who was a sister of Severence Milliken. Her son, Preston, married Lucia Smith, Kelvin's daughter. Kelvin made his effort at a meeting at the Union Club. He said if I stopped at the Club after the meeting we could get together and he would tell me what happened. When we met, he said that the proposal had failed. The indication was again that Severence Milliken didn't agree.

Sometimes the families of the founders of the foundations stayed in Cleveland for a generation or so, but ultimately ended up in other cities and thus the foundation grants were made where they had their new interests, rather than in the donor's city.

In my own case, I served at George Dively's behest, as noted earlier in this book, on the Dively Foundation. Because of my long friendship with him, I knew exactly what he wanted to do with his foundation grants. Simply put, he wanted to make the grants produce additional grants, much like the Corporate 1% Program which started small and grew when others joined. Thus, you could look at the original grants as sort of "seed grants" that blossomed into trees. George Dively knew that I understood that process and I'm certain that's one of the reasons he wanted me to be a trustee of the Dively Foundation.

But Michael Dively, the son of George, didn't see it that way. He wanted to give away the money as fast as possible and get out of the business of running a foundation. I suppose I could have tried to fight for what George really wanted, but I chose not to do that. I'm certain that this scenario has been repeated hundreds of times.

As Kelvin Smith commented to me one day, the sons of self-made prominent men are often estranged from their fathers.

No book on philanthropy in the 50 years we're covering, would be complete without some mention of the affect of the Cleveland Foundation, which during that time was either the largest community foundation in the nation, or at times, the second largest. The total funds of the Cleveland Foundation grew substantially over this period and reached more than $1 billion. Officers and board members of the Foundation changed often and substantially during the period. One of the rules which we found very difficult during the many, many campaigns during this period which were conducted for bricks and mortar, was that the foundation said that it didn't have very much of the total funds available for "capital," and in that way they substantially limited the gifts to these campaigns.

What we tried to do was contact the various board members who also changed over the years, but usually included corporate leaders, to support various requests. In the early years, these trustees or board members had to vote on numerous proposals which had to be read and made the board membership a very difficult job. Later, this task was turned over to the staff of the foundation and thus, the staff became more powerful. The corporate members were not supposed to lobby the other members but I remember specifically that Tom Mastin, the chairman of Lubrizol who became a board member along the way, told me that he diligently tried to conform to that rule, but he found out that he was the only one who was doing so. So he told me that if I wanted him to lobby the other members (from that day on) he would do so. There was always some undercurrent that the Cleveland Foundation grants should not go to the major institutions of Cleveland, but rather to other purposes such as those who wanted to found new institutions or for support of areas that didn't have any connection with major monied interests. I understood these political maneuverings and lived with them, but I always felt that the major institutions in a city are tremendously important to the overall health of the city and should be kept strong. I lean more toward the Kresge Foundation philosophy (Kresge is located just outside Detroit) which would allow an institution to apply for a major grant after it had succeeded in getting a substantial portion of its goal but was still lacking 100% success. I also felt that the Cleveland Foundation was "husbanding" too much of its money, which is also a problem with colleges and universities. The basic argument is that if you are just growing the total endowment, you're not using the money to do good. Sometime in the '80's, I talked with Dick Pogue, who was a very influential member of the Cleveland Foundation board, and said that I thought they ought to be spending more of the Cleveland Foundation money, and he said that at that time they had come to the same conclusion and had set aside a substantial amount of money to cover certain areas. However, I should add that the Cleveland Foundation deserves all the accolades we can give them for trying to do a very important and complicated job. Stu Harrison also presided over the Cleveland Foundation board when they made a major philosophical change and hired Steve Minter to lead them into their present operating mode.

There is also a geographic problem related to the Cleveland Foundation, although they've taken some steps to address it. Institutions in the eastern part of the Cleveland area have a very difficult time getting Cleveland Foundation grants.

The second largest foundation in the Cleveland area is the Gund Foundation, which is a private foundation which has distributed its gifts over the years to institutions where the Gund family has an interest. Colin Baldwin, who was chairman of Sherwin Williams, to whom I became very close because of our work in connection with the major St. Luke's campaign, told me a very interesting story about George Gund. Colin said that this story was told to him by the vice president of Cleveland Trust, which, along with National City Bank, was a major bank in Cleveland. George Gund was head of the Cleveland Trust Bank because of his enormous wealth which made up the large portion of the bank assets. Colin said that *Fortune* magazine wanted to do a major story on George Gund and after prolonged negotiations, George agreed to have it done, but he said that he wanted to see a copy of the story before they printed it in *Fortune*. And *Fortune* agreed. When the story was done, they presented it to the bank's vice president in charge of public relations who took it to George Gund to have him approve it. But the vice president said that as soon as George saw that they had mentioned the fact that one of the early pillars of the Gund family assets was the ownership of a brewery, George said, "You'll have to have them take that out." (He apparently was embarrassed with that part of his family background.) The vice president talked to *Fortune* magazine and told George that *Fortune* said they had agreed to have George read the story before publication but not to change it. George was adamant and said, "I don't want that story printed with the brewery in there!" And the vice president said, "The only way you can get them to take that out of the story would be to have you buy *Fortune* magazine." George pounded the table and said, "That's it!" The end of the story, according to Colin, was that the possible action got back to *Fortune* and the story never ran.

George Gund was a very interesting man. Various people in Cleveland have told me this story about George Gund but I did not hear it from him personally: Apparently when he was a young man his father told his that he should buy insurance. And George thought it over and came to the conclusion that if insurance was such a good buy, the insurance company would be even better, so he invested in insurance companies and that was a part of his very substantial wealth.

Those of us who were top administration at Case would often host various prominent leaders who were attending our various functions. As noted elsewhere, I often hosted Jim Lincoln, and several times I hosted George Gund. These functions usually started at about six o'clock. I found that George Gund would walk out from his office in downtown Cleveland all the way to Case. Many times he was unshaven and somewhat disheveled but sometimes I attended affairs where he would be in a formal tuxedo and he was anything but disheveled – a very handsome man. As noted before, he had the reputation of being quite tough and sending various leaders out of his office with their tails between their legs – especially if they were asking for money from the Gund Foundation. But there had to be another side to George Gund. One time when I had a photograph taken at one of the downtown photographic studios, I noticed a very handsome portrait of George Gund hanging on the wall. And I said to the photographer who owned this little photographic business, "Why the portrait of George Gund?" And he said, "I have nothing but respect for George Gund. He came into my shop and we talked a bit and I happened to mention that my brother was starting a construction business in the East and George Gund asked if he needed money to start the business? And I said, "Yes." Whereupon George Gund said he could arrange to get my brother enough capital to get started, which he did. And my brother is very successful."

The Gund Foundation often teams up with the Cleveland Foundation to make grants.

One of the most successful and long-time executives of the Gund Foundation was Jim Lipscomb. I think, more than most of the other executives of major foundations, Jim seemed to have an inordinate impact on many of the important things that were happening in Cleveland.

He was especially helpful in financing the Yardstick Project.

One day, however, when I was having lunch with Jim, he said to me, "Many people think, Jim, that I have a lot to say about the gifts from the Gund Foundation, but that isn't true." He said, "What I actually do is have a stack of cards at each of the meetings when we have to make decisions on proposals and on the cards I have the pertinent information about each proposal. I turn the cards over one at a time and if no family member raises an eyebrow, I just go on to the next card."

Cleveland and the Cleveland area, is very fortunate because of the great number of family foundations located in the area, such as the 1525 Foundation (Kent and Thelma Smith) and its outgrowth, the Second Foundation, the Kelvin and Eleanor Smith Foundation, the several Humphrey Family Foundations, the Mandel Foundations, the Bruening Foundation, and a number of other foundations including the Reinberger Foundation.

Another important foundation is the GAR Foundation, which started in Akron as a result of the Galen Roush estate, which at first gave only in the Akron area, but as Akron and Cleveland have grown together in their interests, GAR makes gifts throughout the entire area.

I believe we received the first Cleveland gift from the Kresge Foundation which was made when I was at Case. And I think the second grant from Kresge came when I was a consultant at St. Luke's. Later we received a grant when I was a consultant at Beechbrook. Some of the grants resulted from the fact that David Swetland roomed with the chairman of the board of the Kresge Foundation, Bill Baldwin, in college, and we were able to appeal on a personal basis through him. The St. Luke's gift came because of its Methodist background and because we were able to get the Bishop of the Methodist Church to intervene in St. Luke's behalf. The Kresges were Methodist and had rather strict rules about their gifts. One of them was that the requesting institution had to be free of deficits for the last five years before the grant request. Before sending the trustees up to talk with the foundation, I always made very certain that the "askers" knew all of the rules. In connection with a Beechbrook request, Ed Bartlett, who had been head of the trust department of the Cleveland Trust and was a very respected financial man, was part of the group which went up to Kresge in Beechbrook's behalf. When he came back he reported with great chagrin that he had "goofed" and that his goof was going to cost Beachbrook substantially. Apparently, everything went well until one of the Kresge executives asked the question, "Has Beachbrook had any deficits for the last five years?" And the group, remembering our proprietary session said, "No." But Ed, in a moment of banker-type "recollection" said, "Of course if we depreciated our buildings, we would have substantial deficits." Hardly any institutions in the non-profit area depreciated their buildings but the Kresge executive said, "Well Mr. Bartlett, if you believe that the buildings should be depreciated and that this would create a deficit, we just can't make a gift to Beechbrook."

Ed Bartlett was a handsome man and looked, in my opinion, just the way a prominent banker should look. But because he felt so chagrined about his "goof" in connection with Beechbrook, I got to know him a lot better than I would have otherwise. He told me that one of the secrets of his life, which he hoped would never see the light of day, was that in his early career he was a "song and dance man." (I certainly couldn't visualize him with a straw hat, a cane, and a seersucker coat.) And I didn't think that he had any reason to be embarrassed about that, but he was. And it really underscores the fact that "it's the little things in life that mean the most." I tried to convince him that his "goof" would not, in the final analysis, influence the success of the Beechbrook campaign, but I don't think I was every successful. The campaign was successful.

Mentioned earlier, another major national foundation grant in this period was the $9 million grant to Case from the Ford Foundation, which resulted from their effort to influence engineering education nationally. One interesting adjunct to that gift was that one of the Ford Foundation trustees was a friend of Case Institute but suggested that he would not be part of our effort in making that proposal because he could be more helpful if it was not known that he was a friend of Case and could, therefore, vote at the right time without seeming to have a bias.

Another interesting story about that grant is that we actually asked Ford for $15 million, but got a $9 million grant which Ford said would be paid if we raised the $15 million that we had requested. They also said that if we raised the $15 million (which we did), they would consider giving us the other $6 million from our original request. But we never asked for the additional $6 million because

James C. Hardie

Bob Morse, who was president of Case at that time, had been undersecretary of the Navy when Robert McNamara was secretary of defense. They didn't get along at all, and Bob Morse refused to ask the Ford Foundation for the other $6 million (which we had qualified for) because by that time McNamara was head of the Ford Foundation and Bob wouldn't talk to McNamara.

Of course, there are hundreds, indeed thousands, of foundations in the country, and many times during the 50 golden years, trustees of institutions I was consulting with, pressured me to seek grants from those national foundations. But I had found that national foundations really aren't national, although they claim to be; they really make grants in the areas where they're located much like the Cleveland Foundation makes grants in Cleveland. If you mounted a program to seek funds from these national foundations, in my opinion it was a waste of time. If you didn't know anybody at the foundation, you'd get a quick refusal. If you sought someone who had a personal contact with one of the national foundation trustees, that took an inordinate amount of time, and also, usually, ended up with a refusal. So my answer always was, "Let's spend the time more meaningfully here in our own area." And I still think that that is the right approach.

In order to try to put to rest the idea that a great deal of money could be gotten from national foundations, we decided to do a little research project at Case. We hired the head of one of the smaller national foundations, put him on the staff, and then sent him around the country to talk to a group of national foundations, always tailoring our requests to their supposed interests. In each case he was easily able to get a good hearing with the foundations and the proposals were subsequently presented. Over the next six months or so, even though he reported that he had received good hearings, and the chances of our getting the grants were really good, one by one, we received answers and they were all negative.

A few of the scores of campaigns I was connected with stand out in my memory. The Girl Scouts' (1983) was one of the most unique. At the time they asked me to handle the campaign, the director of the Girl Scouts was leaving and there was no one to do the things in a campaign that a director would do. They assigned a new temporary director from out of town. But in some sort of an in-house crisis, they removed all of the board members and replaced them with women who had few top-level contacts. I concluded that the totally new board, the director leaving, and a new temporary director would make a campaign almost impossible. But I thought that 4,000 girls should have some sort of representation, and in talking this over with Dick Kelso, then chairman of East Ohio Gas, both of us came to the conclusion that something ought to be done for those 4,000 Girl Scouts. And he said, "Jim if you take the job I'll find some way to help out." I agreed. At that time he had a great number of other things that he was doing so he started to go into the office at four-thirty in the morning, get his work done for East Ohio Gas, and then spend the rest of the day working for agencies like the Girl Scouts. I think this was one of the greatest examples of philanthropic leadership that I had ever witnessed. Also, he had an employee who kept a book listing all his appointments. She would ride along with him when he had to go to the airport or go to a meeting and they would work out his schedule. We went on with the campaign (1985-1986) and it was a success. Even under the worst circumstances, there is always hope.

All campaigns are somewhat memorable, but another campaign which stands out because of its unusual nature is the Cleveland Playhouse campaign (1981-1982), which started out as a $6 million effort, was increased to $9 million when the internationally known architect, Philip Johnson, was hired, grew to $12 million, because nobody could say "no" to Johnson, and ended up at about $15 million.

Another "stand-out" would be the $16 million Museum of Natural History campaign, which was successful and included almost perfect classic phases of a campaign: 1) Phase I covering the top 100 - - 75% of the goal; 2) Phase II covering the next 400 - - 20% of the goal; and 3) a public phase covering the remainder of the potential prospects - - 5% of the goal. The projected "needed" gifts and those actually received are documented in the Library's archives.

James C. Hardie

The $8 million Western Reserve Historical Society Library campaign (1978-1981) is also of interest because of its "stop and go" scenario.

The records of development efforts at many other institutions to which I was a consultant are archived at the Western Reserve Historical Society, and scholars and professionals might find them of interest. Most conducted major campaigns while I was a consultant. They include: Case Western Reserve University Law School 1967; St. Lukes Hospital 1970; Interracial High School Scholarship Campaign 1970; Lake Erie College Equestrian Center 1971-1974; Dyke College 1972; Ohio College of Podiatric Medicine 1973; Cleveland Health Education Museum 1973; Fairview General Hospital 1975; Morley Library, Painesville 1977; Beechbrook 1977; Holden Arboretum 1978-1979; Hawken School 1978-1980, 1992-1993; Hillcrest Hospital campaign 1979; Wade Park Manor 1979; Laurel School 1980-1982; the Salvation Army 1981-1982; Cleveland Garden Center 1981-1982; Grand River Academy 1981-1982; Ursuline College 1981-1983; Western Reserve Academy 1982-1983; Geauga Hospital 1983-84; Judson Park 1984-1985; Cleveland YMCA 1984-1985; New Directions 1984-1986; St. Vincent Hospital 1985-1986; St. Luke's Hospital (2nd campaign) 1985-1987; Lake Erie College 1986; Council on World Affairs 1986-1987; Old Trail School 1988; Hathaway Brown 1989; Lake County YMCA 1989-1990; Breckenridge Village 1990; Notre Dame-Cathedral Latin School 1991; New Cleveland Campaign 1992-1993; Visiting Nurse Association 1992-1993; Elyria Methodist Home 1992-1993; Regina Health Center 1993; Notre Dame College of Ohio; and Rainbow Babies and Children's Hospital, 1994.

All these records include additional philanthropic leaders who deserve to be remembered. A partial list includes: Mrs. David Ford, Al Pike, Joe Harnett, Dudley Taw, Bruce Griswold, Larry Hatch, Ed Brandon, Pat O'Brien, Charles Bolton, Bob Ginn, Jack Gherlein, Jim Stover, Art Baldwin, Pat Auletta, Ray Armington, Bob Cull, Ralph Besse, Leonard Skeggs, David Swetland, George Humphrey III, Bob Klein, Art Dougan, Wade Harris, Mrs. Harold

Clark, Chloe Oldenberg, Betty Augustus, Liv Ireland, Mort Mandel, Dick Tullis, John Donnell, and Elllery Sedgewick.

Also, there are records at the Historical Society Library of more than 100 meetings and unofficial consultations with more than 100 agencies and institutions.

Summation

I think there is no doubt that when you look at the 50 golden years of philanthropy, which flamed bright in Cleveland in the last half of the 20th century, one must reach the conclusion that a fortunate group of factors are necessary for the type of success which was achieved. I chose to move to Case because I recognized that Cleveland's philanthropic potential was not equaled or duplicated in our nation, and I had the skills and experience to tap this unusual mutation of Fortune 500 corporations, family foundations, individual wealth and exemplary institutions with local leadership epitomized and influenced by Fred Crawford. As Eldon Winkler (now deceased), wrote me at the time of Fred Crawford's one hundredth birthday: "How fortunate we were to have the genius, Fred Crawford, to work with much of the time we were connected with philanthropy."

An important factor was that we were able to convince volunteers to accept the idea of "asking" for a specific gift in a personal solicitation. Also, we convinced corporations to give based on comparative statistics. Sometimes we divided the amount sought from corporations (relative to the campaign goal) according to their sales. Sometimes we related it to the number of their employees. Other times we related it to their profits, but the key to the entire process was that a small group of top corporate leaders accepted the fact that a share of the total campaign goal should be divided equitably among their corporations. With individuals and foundations, the important factor was that the volunteer solicitors accepted the idea that asking a specific sum spread over a certain number years, three in most cases, was proper (a "pledge" rather than a one-time gift).

I would quote a statement by John D. Rockefeller, Jr. about "evaluations" to the volunteer solicitors to explain this approach:

> "Another suggestion I liked to have made to me by a solicitor, is how much it is hoped I will give. Of course such a suggestion can be made in a way that might be most annoying. I do not like to have anyone

tell me when it is my duty to give. There is just one man who is going to decide that question, who has the responsibility of deciding it, and that is myself. But I do like a man to say to me, 'We are trying to raise X millions of dollars and are hoping you may be desirous of giving blank dollars.' If you see your way clear to do so, it will be an encouragement. You may have it in mind to give more. If so, we will be glad. On the other hand, you may feel that you cannot give as much in view of other responsibilities. In that case, we shall understand. Whatever you give after thinking the matter over carefully, in light of our need, your other obligations, and your desire to do your full share as a citizen, will be gratefully received and deeply appreciated."

Because of leaders like Fred Crawford, Charlie Spahr, Charlie White, Kent and Kelvin Smith, "pledging" was embedded in Cleveland, especially among people who controlled much of the wealth. Their leadership, in turn, affected the giving of people all the way down the line. The "Top 100" philosophy wherein we asked the 100 top prospects to give 75% of the total of a campaign, the next 400 to give about 20%, and all the other hundreds of givers to provide the last 5% provided a structure for success. The amount of the first ten or so givers in major campaigns which occurred in this half century was also critical. We knew that campaigns develop from the "inside out." Often, <u>one</u> exemplary gift initiated the process. Kent Smith's $4 million matching gift to the $8 million Museum of Natural History campaign, is an example. This was "revolutionary" giving at a time when million dollar gifts in the nation were only a handful. From a corporate standpoint, exemplary giving through Lubrizol, Sohio, Republic, and especially Fred Crawford's leadership through TRW, set a pattern for the entire community.

Whether another Fred Crawford will emerge is doubtful. Now, concentration on government giving, rather than the private sector, seems to me to be a negative factor. The trends toward a social welfare state, in my opinion, will tend to blunt the great philanthropic achievements which have been evident in Cleveland and in our nation. Fred Crawford always supported "progress" even when it seemed to be a questionable type of progress, so perhaps I'm wrong.

In any event, we still have his legacy -- past, present, and future.

Individuals Mentioned in the Book

Abrams, Frank
Adams, Ansel
Alstadt, Don
Armstrong, Arthur S.
Arnoff, Leonard
Arter, Charlie
August, Harry
Augustus, Betty
Babin, Victor
Bailey, Walter
Baird, John
Baker, Dick
Baldwin, Art
Baldwin, Colin
Bartlett, Ed
Bays, Margaret
Bernard, Lowell
Besse, Ralph
Biggar, Jim
Blair, Claude
Bolten, Francis Paine
Bowen, Bill
Bowes, Fred
Brandon, Ed
Brown, Willard
Cantlin, Brian
Chamberlain, Elizabeth
Churchill, Winston
Clapp, Roger
Clark, Harold
Clegg, Lee
Colkett, Meredith
Colwell, Arch

Congden, Sid
Coolidge, President
Crawford, Kay
Culley, Kathy
Denowski, Thadeous
Dively, George
Donnell, John
Donnell, Otto
Doolittle, Jimmy
Dougan, Art
Dunlap, Jim
Eaton, Cyrus
Eisenhower, Dwight
Emerson, Sam
Eppig, Ruth
Fabyan, Ted
Fairbank, Bob
Fangboner, John
Feighan, Lynn
Fissinger, Bill
Ford, Alan
Ford, Henry
Foster, Claude
Frohring, Paul
Gillespie, Kingsley
Ginn, Bob
Girdler, Tom
Glennan, Keith
Gries, Bob
Gund, George
Hadden, John
Hahn, Edgar
Halvorson, Newt

Hargett, Bill
Harris, Wade
Harrison, Stu
Harrison, Sue
Higley, Ab
Hodge, Jim
Holden, Art
Horn, Charles
Humphrey, George
Humphrey, Lulu
Hunt, Herold
Hunt, Percy
Ingalls, Jr., David
Ingalls, Sr., David
Ireland, R. Livingston
Irrgang, Bill
Jacobs, Dick
Jeffries, Zey
Johnson, Philip
Joseph, Frank
Joseph, Jim
Joseph, Martha
Ketchum, Carlton
Khrushchev, Premier
Klein, Bob
Knight, Jack
Knight, Jim
Land, Ed
Latkovich, Mick
Lennon, Fred
Lester, Tom
Lincoln, Jim
Lindseth, Elmer
Lindseth, Jon
Linowitz, Sol
Lipscomb, Jim
Lord, Tom

MacElroy, Neil
Mandel, Mort
Markley, Herb
Marks, Michael
Martens, Sue
Mastin, Tom
Mattie, Bill
Mavec, Ellen Stirn
McCuskey, George
McDaniel, A. C.
McNamara, Robert
McVey, Bill
Mergler, Harry
Milbourne, Frank
Miller, Sam
Millikan, Severance
Millis, Jack
Mills, Joe
Moll, Theo
Morgenthaler, David
Morgenthaler, Lindsay
Morse, Bob
Moses, Cam
Mueller, Scott
Murch, Boynton
Murphy, John
Napoli, August
Nash, Lucia Smith
Nason, Alex
Noll, Darwin
Norweb, Emory Mae
Norweb, Henry
Nunan, Kneeland
Offett, Molly
Oldenberg, Chloe
O'Neal family
Ong, John

Pace, Stan
Packard, David
Paine, Elliot
Pike, Al
Pike, Kermit
Pogue, Dick
Ramsdell, Bob
Reavis, Jack
Reid, Donna
Reinberger Brothers
Robbins, Fred
Rockefeller, III, John D.
Rockefeller, John D.
Rockefeller, Jr., John D.
Roush, Galen
Roush, Ruth
Rubinstein, Arturo
Salk, Jonas
Scalzi, Pat
Scheele, Bill
Schneider, Hubert
Sears, Lester
Sears, Ruth
Sherwin, Sr., John
Sherwin, John
Shurter, Bob
Sister Henrietta
Skeggs, Leonard
Smith, Eleanor
Smith, Kelvin
Smith, Kent
Smith, Thelma
Smith, Vincent
Spahr, Charles
Sparks, Frank
Spock, Benjamin
Stirn, Cara Smith

Stirn, Howard
Stouffer, Gordon
Stouffer, Vernon
Strawbridge, Herb
Strnad, Bud
Strnad, Edna
Struchen, Maury
Sumerladd, Mrs.
Szubski, Jim
Taw, Dudley
Taylor, Sr., Tom
Thomas, Betty
Thomas, Ed
Timken, Bob
Timken, Mrs. Bob
Timken, Henry
Tippit, Carlisle
Tippit, Hassel
Tormey, John
Toth, Bob
Treuhaft, Bill
Trupo, Stan
Tullis, Dick
Tuve, Lou
Twining, Dave
Warner, Jake
Watson, Tom
Weatherhead, Jr., Albert
Weaver, Paul
Weber, Ron
White, Charlie
White, Margaret Bourke
Willis, Ted
Wilson, Joe
Winkler, Eldon
Wright, Dave
Zeising, Eleanor

Printed in the United States
30591LVS00001BA/22-48